Andrew Bibby is a freelance writer and journalist, who has written for *The Observer*, the *Independent* and other newspapers and magazines. He is the author of a number of outdoor travel books including *The Backbone of England*. He is also the author of a children's novel *Me, Mick and M31*.

His family's links with Purbeck date back to 1918, when his grandfather, stationed in an army camp in Swanage, was taken with the beauty of the countryside around him. His family returned to Purbeck regularly thereafter, and Andrew Bibby has continued this tradition with his own family. He has walked all the walks included in this book several times, and brings a fresh perspective to Purbeck that should delight both residents and visitors alike.

WALKING IN PURBECK

15 Circular Walks

Andrew Bibby

Colour photographs by David Bailey

THE DOVECOTE PRESS

I dedicate this book to the memory of my mother
MARJORIE SAUNDERS BIBBY
who also walked in Purbeck
and wrote of what she found

Fully revised colour edition 2010
First published in 1989 by The Dovecote Press Ltd
Stanbridge, Wimborne Minster, Dorset BH21 4JD

ISBN 978-1-904-34980-8

Text © Andrew Bibby 1989 and 2010
Photographs © David Bailey 2010
Ordnance Survey mapping © Crown Copyright
Map (pages 8/9) © Media4 Graphix Ltd

Andrew Bibby has asserted his rights under the Copyright, Designs and
Patent Act 1988 to be identified as the author of this work

Printed in Spain by GraphyCems, Navarra

All papers used by The Dovecote Press
are natural, recyclable products made from
wood grown in sustainable, well-managed forests

A CIP catalogue record for this book is available
from the British Library

1 3 5 7 9 8 6 4 2

CONTENTS

Introduction 6

THE WALKS:

INTRODUCTION

In Purbeck, it's easy to enjoy walking. Of course, the area has many other attractions, and if you're here on holiday I wouldn't necessarily want to drag you away from the beaches at Swanage and Studland all the time. But it would be a shame to visit Purbeck and not see something of the countryside, and there's no doubt that the best way to do this is on foot. Fortunately, that's not difficult: there is a comprehensive network of rights of way, most of which are easy to find and follow.

Purbeck offers startling contrast in a relatively small geographical area, as you'll appreciate if you explore even a handful of the walks in this book. There's the long ridge of chalk hills, running coast-to-coast from Ballard Point to Worbarrow Bay. There's the coast itself, with high cliffs, little coves and, of course, fine sea views. There's the quiet valley of the Corfe river, and the limestone ridge from Swyre Head to Gad Cliff. And there's also the areas of beautiful heathland.

Fifteen walks means that you can tackle one each day of a two-week holiday, and still have one left for another visit. I've opted for variety, and have tried to include some walks which explore lesser-known parts of Purbeck as well as the obvious favourites. Don't feel compelled to follow the walks slavishly. If you have young children or just fancy a short stroll, then feel free to walk just part of the way. Alternatively, if you're a keen walker and feel let down that the longest walk here is a measly nine miles or so, then tackle two or three together.

The walks are circular and begin and end in towns or villages. I try to indicate what facilities are available to the tired or hungry walker in each place, and whether the routes are serviced by public transport (mostly they are). I also give some idea of the length of each walk, though treat the mileage distances with some caution. Two miles of up-and-down clifftop walking (as near Arish Mell, for example) easily equals three miles of heathland walking. The same applies to time: where one person might stride, another might stroll or even stop for a picnic.

Having been in print for over twenty years, *Walking in Purbeck* may now perhaps be turning into something of a local landmark in its own right; if so, it is a reflection both of the enduring beauty of the area and of the continuing popularity which walking enjoys. But for this new edition, I have approached the book as if for the first time. I have taken the opportunity to introduce two new walks and to make significant changes to two or three of the other walks, in order to cover aspects and areas of Purbeck which I felt were previously under-represented. Even where the walks remain unchanged, the detailed descriptions and instructions for them have all been carefully checked and revised where necessary. Nevertheless the countryside is a living place, and there may well be further changes which take place during the lifetime of this edition: bear in mind, therefore, that not every landmark mentioned will necessarily remain always the same.

Of the changes which recent years have brought, the balance is, I think, a positive one for walkers. The rights of way network in Purbeck is better waymarked and maintained than it once was, and more is being done by the local authorities to encourage walking. A good range of introductory leaflets are available now in visitor centres. (That doesn't mean, of course, that there aren't still occasional problems: a number of stiles on some of the walks featured in this book, for example, need urgent attention, and there continue to be problems in summer with rights of way obliterated by crops or vegetation.)

Another change for the better is that walkers have access to a number of areas of countryside in Purbeck which were not previously openly available to the public. The Countryside and Rights of Way Act (the 'right to roam' legislation long sought by walkers) has introduced some areas of access land, primarily on the heathland, the coast and the Purbeck Hills. Walk 9, for example, includes a short stretch of access land walking near Creech. The National Trust and the RSPB are also to be commended for their work in creating new paths, several of which feature in this book. And although they didn't make it into the book this time, the recently created paths on Stoborough Heath and Hartland Moor nature reserves extend further the options open to walkers in Purbeck.

Looking down, say, from Ballard Down or the Corfe hill towards Poole and Bournemouth it's tempting to conclude that Purbeck, by some lucky chance, has managed to remain wonderfully unspoilt and free from major development. Nevertheless, as I hope this book will make clear, human activity has left a very profound mark on the landscape. Both in the past and certainly today Purbeck has been the

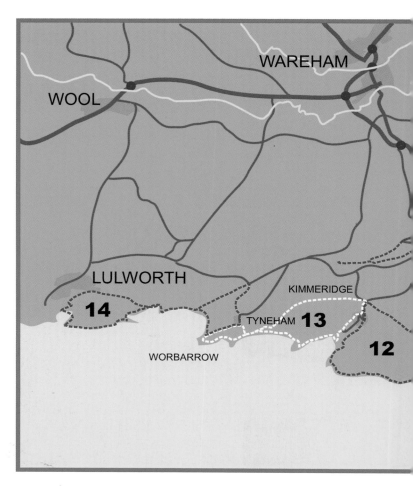

WAREHAM

WOOL

LULWORTH

KIMMERIDGE

14

TYNEHAM **13**

12

WORBARROW

scene of considerable industrial activity – stone, clay, shale and now, most dramatically of all, oil from the massive reserves underneath Purbeck, which are being tapped by BP at their Wytch Farm site. Agriculture, too, as all walkers should remember, is a business: as one Church Knowle resident graphically put it to me once, 'every blade of grass has a price label on it'.

But understanding that Purbeck is a place of economic activity should enhance our understanding and the pleasures to be got from walking, rather than detracting from the experience. I wish you very happy times exploring this wonderful corner of the country.

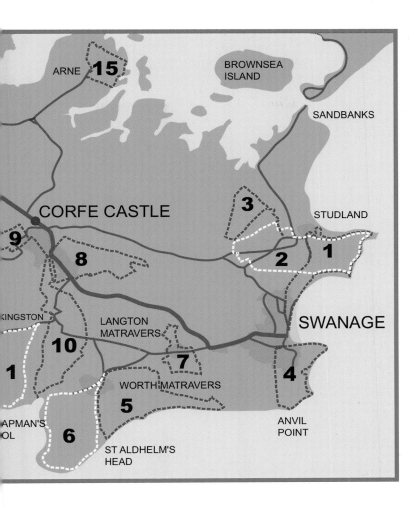

Acknowledgements

Many people have helped me in the preparation of this book. I am particularly grateful to Jane Scullion and to my father Noel Bibby for their many useful comments and suggestions.

I also acknowledge the assistance given, shortly before her death, by Mary Baxter of the Ramblers' Association in Purbeck.

1. THE CLIFFS OF OLD HARRY

Swanage – Old Harry Rocks – Studland – Ballard Down – Swanage

A classic walk of about 5½ miles (8.75 kms) taking 2-4 hours from Swanage beach past the Old Harry Rocks to Studland village, and back across Ballard Down.

STARTING POINT
Swanage beach (New Swanage end). Park in the North Beach car park (at the end of De Moulham Road), or in neighbouring roads. It's sometimes possible to find places to park in or near Burlington Road (off Ulwell Road), in which case a footpath leads directly to the beach.

Buses run along the front between Swanage and Studland and Bournemouth; and to Swanage town from Corfe Castle, Wareham and Poole.

FACILITIES
Studland has a pleasant pub, the Bankes Arms; there are also a number of shops, beach cafes, and several hotels providing meals. Teas often available at Manor Farm. Toilets.

ANY PROBLEMS?
None, although take appropriate care at the cliff edge. The return route back from Studland involves a short, but stiff, climb. Unusually, in certain conditions of tides it may not be safe to begin this walk on Swanage beach, in which case divert via New Swanage.

ABOUT THIS WALK

The Old Harry Rocks used to feature as one of the framed illustrations on the walls of railway compartments, in the days when railway carriages had such things. Nowadays, the pictures have gone and Swanage is no longer part of the national rail

Studland church

network but Old Harry remains a famous Purbeck landmark, rivalling Corfe Castle for a place on the picture postcards and on the cover of travel brochures.

I'm tempted to say that, if you think you only have the time or inclination to do one walk, this should be the one – because I suspect that, having walked around Ballard Point and down to Old Harry, you'll change your mind. Studland is a fine destination for a walk, too. The wonderful sandy beach, a well-situated village pub and the superb unspoilt Norman church should cater for almost all tastes.

Old Harry Rocks pair up with the similar chalk stacks at the Needles, on the Isle of Wight, which are often clearly visible from Swanage. In times past, the chalk downs used to continue unbroken across what is now the English Channel, and Poole Harbour and the Solent were simply a river valley. The sea, having very successfully separated Wight from the mainland still nibbles away at Old Harry. One of the stacks, which had been named Old Harry's Wife, was washed away in a storm in 1896; in exchange, the sea periodically separates new stacks from the main body of chalk, so that Old Harry's family stays much the same size from generation to generation.

The path around Old Harry is one of the most popular in Purbeck, and you won't need to worry about getting lost. The cliffs deserve respect, however, and can be dangerous to anyone foolhardy enough to leave the path, as the records in Swanage lifeboat station demonstrate. Reckless holidaymakers are not a new phenomenon; C.E. Robinson in his book *Picturesque Rambles in the Isle of Purbeck* published in 1882 has a story from a few years earlier:

'It occurred to a pair of Londoners, on a visit to Swanage, to try the excitement of a little home alpine climbing. Soon enough they reached the point from which ascent or descent was equally difficult. Dusk rapidly came on, and during the whole night - one of rain and wind - there they stood, hungry and cold, with their backs to the inhospitable rock. A dense mist hid them from view the next morning, but, though not seen, their cries were heard on board the steamer from Poole, and a party of coastguardsmen were sent out in search. But it was late in the afternoon before the two crestfallen victims of this unlucky adventure were rescued, by means of ropes let down from the top.'

But who needs this sort of adventure when the walk itself has so many pleasures to offer?

THE WALK

Walk along Swanage sea-front away from the town along the promenade. When the sea-wall and huts stop, keep on the beach. Just before the final breakwater turn left up a row of steps, and then almost immediately right up some more steps.

You are now on the coast path, which climbs slowly, skirting the cliff edge. There are fine views to be had back over Swanage beach and bay. The path marks the geological transition to the chalk hills by climbing more steeply, and the fields

to the left give way to open downland. Continue on the coast path, reaching the ridgeway path at a series of earthworks.

Carry on along Ballard Down. The path drops quite steeply until Ballard Point is turned, and the first of the chalk stacks come into sight. Directly ahead now are the buildings of Bournemouth, across the water of Poole Bay. Follow the path as it slowly loses height, until finally the last chalk stacks, the Old Harry Rocks themselves, are reached.

The chalk stacks are a refuge for the sea-birds, safe from human interference. The name on the map, St Lucas Leap, commemorates not some miraculous feat of long-jumping by an early Christian saint, but (so the story goes) an unsuccessful jump by a pedigree greyhound called St Lucas which had belonged to a Studland squire, and which had been trying to catch a hare at the time. Alas, the dog was killed; let's hope the hare survived.

The path turns the corner, and shortly afterwards enters a little

Old Harry Rocks

woodland. Studland and its beach lie ahead. After a few hundred metres of dusty walking, on the outskirts of Studland, follow the alternative route of the coast path sharp right, down to the sea. Turn left past a few beach huts, and then at the beach cafe turn inland up the sunken lane to emerge in Studland village beside some toilets. Turn right on to the tarmac road and pass the Bankes Arms and a National Trust car park.

If you want to spend time in Studland, or reach the main beaches, carry on along the road at this point. But to continue the walk, turn left through a gate immediately after the small N.T. car park, beside a little meadow; the churchyard is directly ahead. Enter the churchyard and turn left once the edge of the church is reached, leaving along the tarmac approach road until the village cross is reached.

Studland church is a wonderful unspoilt Norman church, which has been described as one of the dozen or so most complete examples in the country. It seems likely that it was originally built before the Conquest but rebuilt soon afterwards. Incidentally, look out for the carved stone faces – both animal and human – on the external north wall of the nave and the prominent gravestone of Waterloo veteran Sergeant William Lawrence.

For many years, all that was left of Studland's village cross was a stone stump. The cross you see today may look traditional but a closer look will reveal some less conventional images, including one of Concorde. The stone came from a quarry at St Aldhelm's Head and was carved by a local marble-worker Treleven Haysom; the cross itself was erected in 1976.

At the cross keep straight ahead, taking the track past Manor Farm and its outbuildings. The track rapidly becomes tarmac again, and runs ahead up to the Glebeland Estate of houses on the side of the hill. Follow the road passing a number of houses to your right until the road finally peters out. Carry on through a gate, joining an old track which runs diagonally up the side of the hill. The path crosses a meadow before reaching the brow.

Here there is an old much-weathered stone which invites you to 'Rest and Be Thankful'. The stone was erected here in 1852 by David Jardine (his initials can be seen at the side of the stone), a Londoner who also donated a clock to Swanage parish church.

Cross the ridgeway path and continue downhill, the path falling diagonally to the right. Swanage and its bay are now in view again; directly below is Whitecliff Farm. When the path reaches the limits of open downland, carry on through a little gate into a sunken track between two fields. Keep straight ahead at Whitecliff, crossing over the farm approach road.

Whitecliff farmhouse dates back to the early seventeenth century, though the site itself is mentioned in the Domesday Book. 'No more charming site for a house than that of Whitecliff can be found along the sea-coast for many a long mile', wrote C.E. Robinson in 1882. 'Such an aspect - warm, sunny, and sheltered! such beautiful views around! such fine old elms and poplars!'

Cross a stile, and take a narrow path running between two fields until finally a tarmac suburban road is reached. Carry on down Hill Road, turn left, and then follow the road down to the New Swanage corner shop. Here the main road from Studland joins from the right; follow it, initially half-left, back down to the beach.

2. STUDLAND TO BALLARD DOWN (& OLD HARRY AGAIN)

Studland – Ulwell – Ballard Down – Old Harry Rocks – Studland

A six mile (9.5 km) walk taking 2-3½ hours, initially across the heathland and then following the ridgeway path along Ballard Down, returning to Studland past the Old Harry Rocks.

STARTING POINT
Studland village. Buses from Swanage and from Bournemouth, over the toll ferry. Use the National Trust North Beach Car Park, or the smaller car park next to the Bankes Arms.

FACILITIES
In Studland: Bankes Arms pub, shops, beach cafes, hotel meals and teas; toilets. (Studland offers a wonderful sandy beach, and the village itself is worth exploring: see the introduction to Walk 1)

ANY PROBLEMS?
The route is relatively straightforward on the heathland; very straightforward once Ballard Down is reached.

ABOUT THIS WALK

This walk offers both heath and hills, a wonderful combination.

Ballard Down is a particular favourite of mine. I've walked along the springy turf of the ridgeway on fiercely hot days, when the heat haze has danced off the land just ahead of the path, and when the sailing boats in Studland Bay below have been little white dots on a sea of bright blue. Admittedly I've also stood beside the Ulwell obelisk, completely drenched, as the rain whipped in from across Godlingston Hill.

I hope you get the sunshine, but even if the weather is bad there's something to be said for getting out the waterproofs and

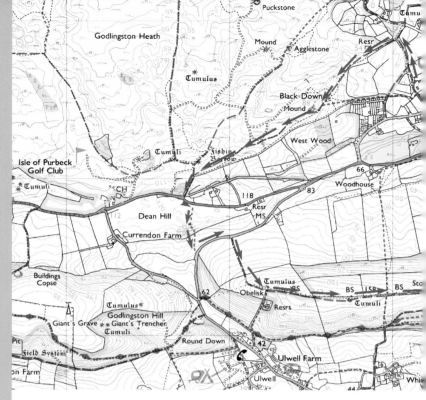

coming this way.

I make no apologies for including again the section of cliff walking around Ballard Point and Old Harry Rocks – if you've done Walk 1, you'll have been this way already, but I'm sure you won't mind repeating the experience.

THE WALK

The walk starts from the cross-roads on the main road in the centre of Studland village, by the village hall. Walk a short distance north along the main road towards the ferry, passing through a little wooded area. Turn left towards Studland stables just before a house named Studholme. Keep to the right of the stables (and to the left of a garage), following the path through a small wood. Cross a stile, and then cut diagonally across a small field, to another stile.

Beyond the stile, turn right along a well-worn sandy lane. The lane skirts to the right of an open pasture (ignore the first bridleway left, across this pasture) before gorse and bracken begin to close in. As

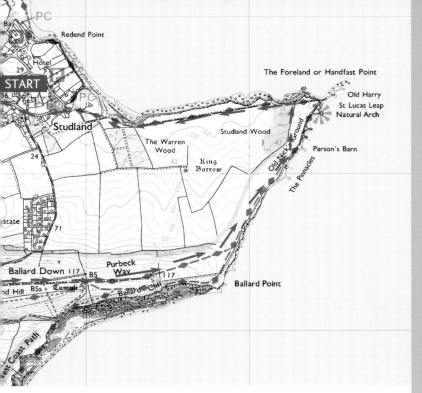

the main track swings towards the right, turn left to climb up a track on to the heathland. The track initially runs up the outside of a field boundary.

Keep straight ahead, ignoring various side-turnings, climbing steadily. The outlying houses in Studland village lie a little way off. To your left, the obelisk on the hill at Ulwell, which the walk reaches in due course, is easy to spot.

As the golf course is approached, it's worth turning back to admire the view over the harbour.

Carry on until the path emerges on to the Isle of Purbeck golf course. Turn sharp left, taking a narrow path between trees and bushes.

Cross the Studland-Corfe road, and climb the stile almost opposite. You are now on the 9-hole golf course. Walk across the fairways aiming for the tallest of the trees opposite; you will find the path disappearing down the hill, through some undergrowth. A stile takes you into a large pasture; head right, to a stile on to the Swanage road.

Walk left along the main road for a couple of hundred metres, turning first right up a track, which climbs the side of the hills. A National Trust sign confirms the route. Carry on up the track to the Obelisk.

The obelisk began life in the city of London, in front of the church of St Mary Woolnoth. Like many other pieces of redundant London masonry it was carefully brought down to Swanage by George Burt (see page 27), and erected on a bronze age barrow at Ulwell to celebrate the construction of Swanage's Ulwell waterworks. This was Burt's second effort to improve his home town's water supply - in 1864 he had obtained an Act of Parliament to raise water from an artesian well, and had built the waterworks at the back of Sentry Road, Swanage. The obelisk was taken down in 1941, as it was considered to be too obvious a landmark for enemy planes. Most of the stone sections were re-assembled by an Army working party in 1973.

The Obelisk, Ballard Down

Swanage from Ballard Down

You will need no detailed instructions for the next part of the walk: the ridgeway path continues along the brow of Ballard Down, with wonderful views on both sides of the hill. Ballard Down was acquired by the National Trust as part of its Enterprise Neptune, and the N.T. has restored the downland turf.

Carry on along the track until Ballard Point and the Old Harry Rocks are reached. (If you have already come this way with Walk 1, you may want to divert just before Old Harry to explore the woodland walks in Studland Wood, just to the left).

Follow the path back towards Studland. Once the tarmac road in the village is reached, turn left and follow the road back to the starting point for the walk.

3. THE AGGLESTONE AND THE HEATH

Studland – Agglestone – Godlingston Heath – Greenland – Studland

A 4½ mile (7.25 km) walk of 1¾-3½ hours from Studland across the heathland, visiting the Agglestone and the Godlingston Heath national nature reserve.

STARTING POINT
Studland village. Use the National Trust North Beach Car Park, or the smaller car park next to the Bankes Arms. Buses (Swanage-Studland-Bournemouth) pass.

FACILITIES
In Studland: Bankes Arms pub, shops, beach cafe, hotel meals; teas; toilets.

ANY PROBLEMS?
Can be muddy in a number of places, especially in wet weather. Generally waymarked but follow the directions with care especially near the golf course.

ABOUT THIS WALK

This walk takes you into the secret part of the Isle of Purbeck, the area of wild heathland which so many Swanage holidaymakers don't discover. They are missing out, for as this walk demonstrates the heath has its own considerable beauty. You won't find many other people on this walk, but you will find some very unspoilt countryside and some fine views. And the Agglestone, reached after only a mile or so, should be on every visitor's itinerary.

The heathland stretches across the northern half of the Isle of Purbeck, bounded by the hidden reaches of Poole Harbour in the north and the hills in the south. In fact, the heath continues beyond Purbeck, becoming the great Dorset heath which Thomas Hardy called Egdon

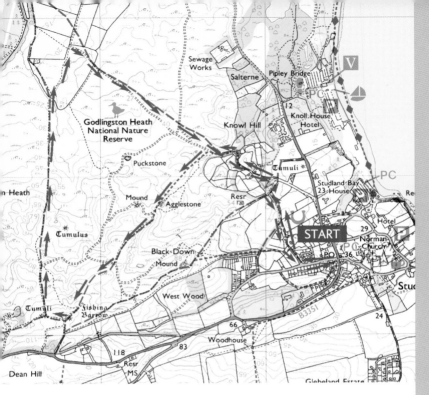

Heath. Hardy used the setting of the heath as atmosphere for some of his novels, and in some places it can seem a brooding place.

The heathland is of considerable interest to naturalists. Many rare plants can be found, including Marsh Gentian, Bog Orchid, and the conspicuously large heather called Dorset Heath, which is mainly confined to the Purbeck area. All six British reptiles live on the Purbeck heathland, including the rare sand lizard and the smooth snake. The adder lives here too – which shouldn't discourage you, though avoid walking through undergrowth in beach sandals.

There are deer nearby as well, particularly in the conifer forestry plantations just to the west. The best time to catch sight of the deer is twilight – but having said that, once as I approached Greenland at the hottest time of a hot May day two little roe deer watched me closely from the shelter of some trees, a short distance away. A little earlier, a solitary fox had emerged on to the path ahead of me, looked me up and down, and sauntered off again. Even if humans are missing, you may share your walk with others.

THE WALK

As for the previous walk, start from the cross-roads on the main road in the centre of Studland village, by the village hall. Walk up Heath Green Rd, with the village hall on your left, for a short way before taking the bridleway on your right just before the children's playing field.

Follow the bridleway for a few hundred metres. (Very briefly you will be on the same route as Walk 2.) Continue as the track swings round to your right, until it is crossed by an unmade dusty road. Turn left at this point, and walk past Wadmore farm and cottages.

Once past the buildings, the road becomes a track through woodland, with a wooden bridge over a stream. Turn left off the bridge. At the edge of the wood, the Agglestone, a large rock perched on a hillock, comes into sight. Turn left off the main path almost immediately, heading off across the heath until you reach the rock.

The Agglestone makes a powerful impression as it rises up above the deserted heathland. It's quite easy to understand how stories grew up locally that it was the work of the devil, whose hand slipped when throwing it from the Isle of Wight intending to demolish Salisbury Cathedral (some say Corfe Castle). In fact, the Agglestone's origins are more prosaic, but nevertheless remarkable: it is a natural phenomenon, being made of hard ironstone and weighing about 500 tons, which has remained in place while the surrounding heath has been eroded over the millennia. Part of the Agglestone's effect comes from its setting. Its name, Agglestone, may mean 'holy stone', or it may mean 'witch stone'.

Carry on past the Agglestone on the main track. At the first waymark stone, several hundred metres beyond, keep broadly straight ahead through a gate, following the sign to Studland road. The path bears a little to the right before emerging alongside a fairway of the Purbeck golf course. When the path arrives at a track at a T-junction, turn right. Shortly afterwards, look for a somewhat inconspicuous stone sign directing you off sharp right towards Rempstone Forest. Take this, and when the path splits almost immediately keep straight ahead following a sign to Greenland.

The next part of the walk is easy to enjoy, with superb views down over the heathland to Poole Harbour and to Poole and Bournemouth beyond.

The Agglestone

It was the landmark National Parks and Access to the Countryside Act passed in 1949 by the post-war Labour government which introduced for the first time the concept of national nature reserves, and the heathland here was one of the first reserves to be designated. This was in 1954, when the heathland was still littered with old munitions from the Second World War and when unexploded ordnance regularly turned up among the heather.

The importance of lowland heathland as a unique habitat is now properly recognised, but only after a great deal of heath has already been lost. Natural England says that England today has only about 20% of the lowland heath it once had, and it's easy to see from this walk why. Much former heathland was swallowed up for housing (as across Poole Harbour, where the conurbation of Bournemouth spreads for miles), and some was planted with conifers (as with the large plantations in Purbeck just to your left). Some heathland was also converted into agricultural land, a fate which befell much of Purbeck's heathland further east (Natural England is currently trying to reverse this in its work on its Stoborough Heath reserve).

Like most of our landscapes, heathland is the result of human interaction with the natural environment. Heathland became established in parts of England as a result of woodland clearances by our ancestors more than 4000 years ago. Thereafter, the heathland habitat was looked after and managed by local communities, who used the resources which it provided: gorse was collected as a fuel (especially for bread ovens), heather was taken for thatching and road building, and turf was cut for burning. The heath itself provided grazing land. It is only in relatively modern times that these uses began to fall off and heathland started being treated simply as waste land.

As well as being a national nature reserve, this stretch of heathland has also been designated as a Site of Special Scientific Interest.

Continue on the track you're on, as the green fields ahead gradually become nearer. This section can be wet underfoot.

Greenland or Greenlands (both single and plural usage seem acceptable) is well named: the green fields contrast with the heather and gorse-covered heathland, from which they were created. Nearby is Newton, named from an abortive attempt in 1286 by Edward I to create a new town on this site, as a rival to powerful Poole across the water. More recently, this area was the scene of a large-scale clay mining operation: a narrow-gauge railway ran to Goathorn peninsula, where boats were loaded with ball clay to be shipped to the Potteries.

It's hard to picture this industrial activity today, but appearances are deceptive. Beneath the heath, and underneath Poole Bay as well, is the massive Wytch Farm oil field, the largest on-shore oil field in Europe.

An initial oil well sunk at Wytch Farm, a little way away on the edge of Poole Harbour, has been joined in recent years by other wells on the heathland. BP are well aware that their operations have to take place in a particularly beautiful and environmentally sensitive area. Comprehensive surveys of the heathland - even to the extent of commissioned maps detailing the location of every Dorset Heath plant – were undertaken and exercises have regularly taken place to test the ability of the authorities to deal with an oil spill in Poole Harbour. However, there is no doubt that the oil industry provides a challenge to Purbeck's status as an area of outstanding natural beauty.

Keep straight ahead (ignoring the track to your left signed to Rempstone) until the first of Greenland's green fields is reached. After a very short distance, you should reach a prominent waymark signpost: turn right here, slightly back, on to another prominent track. (If the waymark has failed to survive by the time you come this way, the track should nevertheless be relatively easy to locate).

The path now runs back across Studland Heath to the point where you turned off to go to the Agglestone. Beyond here, turn back over the wooden bridge, pass Wadmore cottages again, and then turn right on to the bridleway, following it as it bends round to the left to return to Studland village.

4. GREAT NATURE'S OPEN BOOK – DURLSTON

Swanage – Durlston – Anvil Point – Quarries – Swanage

This is a gentle 4 mile (6.5 km) circular walk of 1½-3 hours, from the centre of Swanage to the Durlston Country Park (for the Globe), and back again through old stone quarrying areas.

STARTING POINT
Swanage, by the pier.

FACILITIES
Refreshments at Durlston Country Park.

ANY PROBLEMS?
Very few. This route is popular and easy to follow.

ABOUT THIS WALK

It was in the last decades of the nineteenth century that Swanage underwent a quite profound transformation. What had previously been a working sea-port where the stone trade dominated the local economy found itself changing out of all recognition. 'Trippers' began arriving, both on the trains (the branch line opened in 1885) and by paddle-steamers from newly-developed Bournemouth. The sandy beach became the centre of life and tourism muscled out the stone merchants. Swanage's two piers tell the story: the old pier (now just a set of wooden stumps set in the sea) had been built in 1859 for trade; the new pier, erected in 1896, was for leisure.

One man conveniently links together both sides of this story. George Burt (1816-1894) was a Swanage man who made his fortune in London as a partner in his uncle's stone and building business (his uncle was John Mowlem, the son of a Swanage quarryman and the founder of the famous construction company). Burt was familiar with the old Swanage, the one where stone was brought down to the town from the quarries of Herston and Langton, stored beside the water in stone stacks or 'bankers', and then carried in carts by horses into the shallow waters of the bay, ready to be transferred into small boats. These boats in turn conveyed the stone further out to sea, where sailing ships would be riding at anchor waiting to receive their cargo. Later, of course, the construction of the pier meant that ships could tie up there, with the stone taken to them along the tramway from the bankers.

But if Burt knew Swanage as it had been, he also had a major part in the making of the new, visitor-orientated, town. Having built his business and made his money by paving London's streets with Purbeck stone, he then set about doing his best to improve his home town in best Victorian style. He laid out his Durlston estate with wide avenues and promenades, with seats suitably positioned for admiring the vistas and with stone signs, appropriately inscribed with exhortations ('Look round, and read Great Nature's open Book').

Burt had a strong educational streak: stone plaques were put up on the side of Durlston Castle to inform visitors, among other things, of the duration of the longest day at Spitsbergen, the convexity of the oceans, and the height of spring tides at Swanage.

Durlston went through a torrid time in the second half of the twentieth century: Burt's great globe, for example, was fenced off behind turnstiles and became a rather tacky tourist attraction. The terraced walkways became overgrown. Burt's 'Castle' was a lost building in search of a new role, at various times a tired cafe or unprepossessing bar.

It has been the designation in 2001 of the Dorset and East Devon coastline, the Jurassic Coast, as a UNESCO world heritage site which has helped save Durlston and led to its transformation. Lottery and other grant funding is ensuring that Burt's Durlston Castle can have a second lease of life as one of the main visitor centres for the heritage coast. New interpretation boards are going up, to complement Burt's old plaques. The old man, now resting in the cemetery in Kensal Green in London, would, you feel, have been delighted.

THE WALK

From the pier, follow the 'coast path' sign to the right of the Swanage Sailing Club and make your way towards Peveril Point, either along the shoreline (which can be slippery) or along Peveril Road, just above.

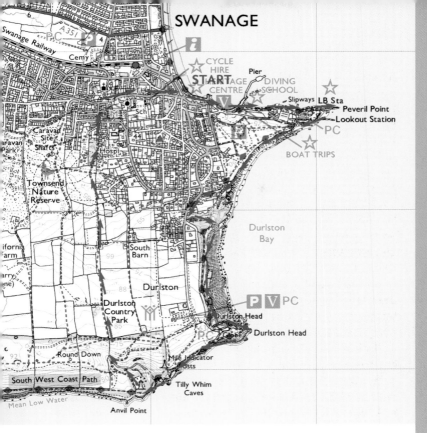

SWANAGE

Peveril is still one of the most pleasant parts of Swanage, and the centre of the small lobster fishing industry. As you walk to the point, there's a chance to admire the clock tower, a typical piece of Victorian gothic architecture which was originally erected near London Bridge to commemorate the Duke of Wellington. Unfortunately his tower was soon found to hold back the London traffic - whereupon John Mowlem's firm dismantled it and shipped it to Swanage. The clock tower (the clock itself never arrived at Swanage) is one of a number of relics from London which Mowlem and Burt were responsible for bringing here. Their motives must have been partly pragmatic, since the masonry helped provide ballast for the otherwise empty stone boats on the return journeys.

The lifeboat station has been a landmark in this part of Swanage since 1875, when a south-east gale and a dark night conspired to drive an Exeter ship, the *Wild Wave*, on to the rocks at Peveril. Fortunately, the crew of five were saved by coastguards, but it was clear that

The Globe, Durlston Castle

they were lucky. The town needed a lifeboat, and got one almost immediately: the story of the rescue appeared in *The Times*, and the next day one of the readers came forward with the money for the boat.

The Swanage lifeboat house is frequently open to visitors, and the main boat itself is a fine sight particularly when being launched down the slipway into the bay. The Purbeck coastline remains treacherous to commercial shipping and the Peveril Ledges which stretch out seawards from Peveril Point need to be given a wide berth.

From the coastwatch lookout at Peveril Point, follow the path uphill along the edge of the cliff. Swanage's second bay, Durlston Bay, is below you; Durlston Castle can be seen ahead at the end of the bay.

The path continues along the cliff-side before leaving the grassy hillside by two stone seats. When you reach a tarmac road, turn left (an old stone sign confirms the way). Continue to the end of the road, turning left when you emerge at the more major Durlston Road. Walk along the road for a short way, and then turn left on to a footpath into woodlands. (This route for the coast path is relatively new, the more direct route having been closed because of cliff erosion problems.) Another left turn will bring you to the edge of the bay, where you pick up the old route of the coast path. The path now wanders through some overgrown woodlands. The woods have been cut back a little recently and a number of viewpoints give glimpses out towards the Isle of Wight.

As the path arrives at Durlston, turn and walk down the right-hand side of the Castle until you reach the stone Globe.

The Globe is, along with Corfe Castle and Old Harry Rocks, a familiar picture on postcards. It was constructed in 1887 in Mowlem's yard at Greenwich from 15 pieces of Portland stone held together by granite dowels, and is estimated to weigh about 40 tons.

The Globe has recently been restored, so that the place names and details can once again be made out. Around it Burt put up a series of tablets quoting the poets, as well as blank stones inscribed 'Persons anxious to write their names will please do so on this stone only'. Also nearby are old London metal bollards: Swanage has over 100 of them in total, rescued by Burt when they were no longer required in the capital.

Take the steps down from the Globe and turn right on to the coast

The Lighthouse, Anvil Point

path, enjoying the fine view straight out to sea. A bracing sea wind often accompanies it, making a pleasant change after the sheltered woodlands of Durlston Bay. Follow this path as it winds along the cliff edge, past the old entrance to the Tilly Whim Caves. The Caves (old stone quarries) are closed to the public due to the danger of rock falls, but can be seen behind you as you leave the Durlston estate path to scramble down, and then back up, a little valley towards the lighthouse.

Beyond the lighthouse on Anvil Point, which was erected in the early 1880s, the coast path continues enticingly. If you have the time and energy, carry on a little further. Thrift, sea plantain and samphire are among the plants and flowers growing here, and the cliffs are home for many types of sea-birds. Enjoy the sea views along the Purbeck coast, before retracing your steps.

Leave the lighthouse and take the tarmac access road for a short distance inland. Immediately after crossing the small whitewashed bridge turn sharp left, to follow a path up the hillside. Bear left at the top, to find a gate.

Pass through the gate, and immediately to your right you'll see another gate, leading into a meadow. This is the start of the path back to Swanage. Enter the meadow (stones set in the wall provide an alternative to the gate), and continue down the right-hand side of the field.

From now on, it is easy walking back to the centre of Swanage. The town itself comes into view shortly on your right, while over to the left is the pocked ground which denotes former quarrying activity. Keep to the path, which runs almost straight ahead.

The track skirts some new houses and becomes tarmac. Carry straight on, and in due course Swanage church tower appears, directly ahead.

You emerge into Townsend Road. Drop down to the High Street, and turn right to retrace your steps to the pier. (Before you do, you may want to take the opportunity of exploring the old Mill Pond area just next to the church).

As you walk back down High Street, notice the frontage of Swanage's Town Hall, another London souvenir saved by George Burt. This was originally the entrance to the Mercers' Hall in Cheapside, London, and dates back to 1670. Across the road from the Town Hall is George Burt's former residence Purbeck House, now a hotel, which not surprisingly has its own curiosities, including statues from London's Royal Exchange and stone balustrades from the old Billingsgate Market.

5. DANCING LEDGE

Worth Matravers – Dancing Ledge – Seacombe – Winspit – Worth Matravers

A relatively straightforward five mile (8 km) walk of 2-3½ hours from Worth Matravers to the coast at Dancing Ledge, and then back along the cliff path to the old quarrying areas at Seacombe and Winspit.

STARTING POINT
Worth Matravers village. Park in the visitors' car park, on the road from Kingston near the Square and Compass pub. Occasional buses from Swanage and Corfe serve the village.

FACILITIES
The Square and Compass is a delightful old Purbeck stone pub, a village local which is also welcoming to visitors. The Worth Tea Rooms provide lunches and teas.

ANY PROBLEMS?
The paths are easy and well marked, and should present few difficulties. May be muddy in places.

ABOUT THIS WALK

One of the delights of Dancing Ledge must be its name. It is the sea that does the dancing, throwing up foam along the smooth flat ledge that juts out into the English Channel. On summer days, it's a pleasant place to sit and relax, watching the passing shipping in one direction and the passing hikers on the Dorset coast path in the other.

Dancing Ledge began life as a quarry, but it's been a favourite place for excursions for generations. On at least one occasion in the past it lived up to its name. William Masters Hardy, a Swanage builder and knowledgeable local historian, wrote a classic book of reminiscences of *Old Swanage, or Purbeck Past and Present*, which was published in 1910. In the book he recounts one particular picnic at Dancing Ledge, attended by the massed ranks of the Swanage Brass and Reed Band. After lunch at one o'clock ('a plentiful repast, consisting of a lobster tea, salad and liquid refreshments'), the band struck up, and dancing took place until the party finally returned to Swanage at six.

Dancing Ledge can only be reached by walking, and traditionally it's approached from Langton Matravers. Cars can be driven down Durnford Drove, a rather cheerless and almost suburban road, as far as Spyway Farm, and then it's a shortish walk across fields to the coastline. My route, from Worth Matravers, is a little further, but in my opinion well worth the extra effort. And finishing at Worth provides an excuse for a drink in the fascinating Square and Compass inn afterwards.

The National Trust now owns much of this land and has added considerably to the pleasures of walking here by creating several new paths, and by erecting neat stone waymarks. The path followed in this route from Eastington Farm to Dancing Ledge is one of these new National Trust paths.

THE WALK

Leave Worth village by heading back along the Langton road, past several houses. Just beyond the Newfoundland Close development, a footpath sign points you right over a stile into a small field. Take this path, cross almost immediately the driveway to Abbascombe House (two more stiles), and then head across the next field, aiming for the far corner. A stile takes you into another field. Keep on the brow, following the path which crosses the field to the left of a stone wall, to arrive in due course at a gate. Keep ahead along a track, passing to the left of Eastington Farm.

The Square and Compass, Worth Matravers

You are now on the Priests Way, the old route followed in mediaeval times when the priests at Worth serviced a daughter church at Swanage (see Walk 7). Eastington Farm itself dates back to the seventeenth century, one of several stone-built farmhouses in Purbeck which have survived from this time. Several of Eastington's original round-headed windows remain in place.

Turn off the Priests Way at the first gate past Eastington Farm. A National Trust stone conveniently confirms the spot. Cross the next field, and go through a gateway at the end. There is now a choice of paths. One track disappears down the valley to Seacombe. Our path, however, turns left and skirts round the brow of the hill, parallel to a boundary stone wall.

From the path, mediaeval farming terraces known as strip lynchets can be clearly seen on the hillside opposite. Strip lynchets were designed to level off the hillsides and make crop-growing easier, and are visible in several parts of Worth parish.

The path turns sharp left and you enter by a stile into another large field, which falls away right towards the sea. Carry along the edge of this field, keeping the stone wall to your left. There are wonderful views over the English Channel: even better, the path conveniently slopes downhill most of the way.

Keep alongside the wall into a second field, and then cross a footpath from Acton to the sea (marked by another N.T. stone). When finally the field ends, take the stile in the corner, and turn inland for a short way.

After only a hundred metres or so, you will reach another waymark stone and stile. Turn right into the neighbouring field and take the path through the gorse which runs off diagonally to the right. When the undergrowth clears, turn left taking the wide grassy track down the hillside. The path leads directly down to Dancing Ledge. If you want to visit the Ledge, cross out of the bottom field and follow the path down to the sea.

As well as its function as a quarry, Dancing Ledge played a useful role in another former element of the local economy. Once again, William Masters Hardy's book is worth quoting (he is describing the years around 1830):

'At one time there were a number of people in Langton and the neighbourhood well known to be great smugglers. One dark night in December they were expecting a cargo of tubs in at Dancing Ledge. The ganger and his men were all on the Ledge watching for their craft. They had not long to wait before she came. They got the tubs ashore all right, and away went the boat to sea again in the darkness.'

However then came the question of what to do with the haul. Overnight the barrels were left at Spyway barn, guarded by the local bull which had conveniently been allowed to roam free that night. But the next day the smugglers moved the cargo to a more secure, and more unlikely, place – in Langton church:

'Most of the smugglers' hiding places had become well known to the Coastguards,' explains Hardy. 'Another place had to be found somewhere. One of the head [smugglers] thought he knew a first-rate place, which was over the ceiling of the church in the apex of the roof . . . reached by going up inside the tower. This new place was used for smuggling for a long time before it was discovered.'

The coast path runs along the south side of the field which you crossed when reaching Dancing Ledge. Follow it along the cliff edge

Dancing Ledge

towards Seacombe, a mile or so away.

At Seacombe, turn inland up the valley for a few hundred metres, following the dusty track. Finally, when the last of the quarried areas is passed, turn left up some steps to continue along the coast path. (At this stage, as a shorter alternative, you could carry on up the valley towards Worth Matravers, though the footpath is not particularly interesting).

At the top of the steps, the path turns left and quickly rejoins the cliff-side. There are fine views back towards the lighthouse at Anvil Point, and this is a good place to see just how extensive the cliff quarries were along all this stretch of coastline. Seacombe and Winspit are two of the largest old quarries, but the sites of others, long unworked, are marked by the strange square-cut caves in the cliffs which can be clearly seen from the coast path.

When the coast path turns left to descend to Winspit, continue ahead on the wide grassy track round the side of East Man hill. The village of Worth comes into view ahead.

Follow the path through a gateway into a second field and here turn half left, immediately entering a third field. Keep straight ahead, to come out at a stile. Now turn right on to a track, and immediately right again to follow the well-walked path across a large field straight back to the cottages at Worth village.

6. THE CHAPEL ON THE CLIFF – ST ALDHELM'S HEAD

Worth Matravers – Winspit – St Aldhelm's Head – Coast path – Worth Matravers

A clifftop walk of just under 5 miles (8 kms) from one of Purbeck's most attractive villages, taking 2-3 hours.

STARTING POINT
Worth Matravers village. As for Walk 5, park in the visitors' car park, on the road from Kingston near the Square and Compass pub. Occasional buses.

FACILITIES
Pub; tea-rooms. (See introduction to previous walk for more about Worth village).

ANY PROBLEMS?
The footpaths are easy to find and well-walked but be prepared for the stiff climb down, and then up, on the stretch from St Aldhelm's Head to Chapman's Pool. In places, the coast path runs very close to the cliff edge.

ABOUT THIS WALK

The maps give you a choice of saints, but there is no doubt that the headland south of Worth Matravers is rightfully named after St Aldhelm, who in the seventh century converted the heathen Purbeck people to Christianity. A surprising amount is known about him: he was born in 735 and was the first Bishop of Sherborne. Several of Purbeck's churches, it is said, may be on the sites of original churches established by Aldhelm. (The little chapel at St Aldhelm's Head itself is not quite so ancient, dating merely from the twelfth century).

You don't need to be a specialist in early church history to enjoy this walk, however. From Winspit to Chapman's Pool is coastal walking all the way, with views to be enjoyed both eastwards towards Durlston

and Dancing Ledge and then - once the headland is turned - to the west, towards Kimmeridge, Worbarrow and the distant shape of the Isle of Portland.

The path along Purbeck's south coast is deservedly popular with walkers. It makes up a section of the South West Coast Path, the longest of the official national trails, which begins just a few miles away at the northern tip of Studland Bay and ends more than six hundred miles later at Minehead in Somerset. In between, walkers have the chance to relish at their leisure the cliffs and coastline of four counties.

THE WALK

From the centre of the village, below the duckpond, turn left past a small row of cottages, London Row, and then take the path into a large field. Cross this field by the well-defined track down the valley. An unmade-up road joins from your right; the track continues downhill, hugging the side of the hill while, to your left, runs an overgrown stream. Shortly after the private track to Winspit Cottage is passed take the coast path to your right, climbing up the side of an old quarry. Look back as you climb for a view down over Winspit Cottage and its walled garden.

Winspit Cottage was the home of one of the last of the quarrymen in this area, William Jeremiah Bower (Billy Winspit to everyone locally), who was almost eighty when he died in 1966. His father, grandfather and great-grandfather had also been quarrymen.

Winspit was one of the places where stone from the coastal quarries was once winched into small boats brought inshore for the purpose, which then had to be rowed back around Anvil Point and Peveril into the relative safety of Swanage Bay. It was a hazardous exercise, as William Masters Hardy in his 1910 book of memories of old Purbeck (see page 33) makes clear: 'It often happened that, when the boat was hauled in under the perpendicular and overhanging cliffs ... and made fast for loading the stone, which was lowered down by means of tackle and cranes, from 90 to 100 feet above, it would sometimes slip from the tackle, and, dashing down with tremendous force, would perhaps just miss the heads of the leading men in the boats, and plunge into the water, almost overwhelming the stone mariners ...'

The boats themselves, heavily laden with stone, could be very unseaworthy: 'It was only frantic and prolonged efforts at bailing and energetic verbal encouragement from the sailors on the vessels close by that would save the boat, crew and stone from sinking and being lost in the depths of that forbidding coast. But sometimes such was the callousness which familiarity with danger bred in the onlookers during such exciting times that, instead of rowing to and assisting the puffing and sweating bailers, these humorous sailors would simply goad on the poor toilers by laughing at them and cracking jokes at their expense'.

The path reaches the coast proper and then hugs the cliff edge,

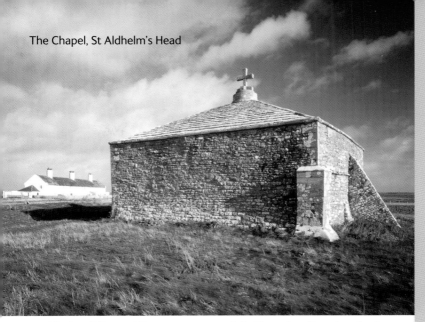

The Chapel, St Aldhelm's Head

with the cliffs tumbling away to your left. There is a fine view back along the coast to the lighthouse at Anvil Point, with the old quarries in the cliffs clearly visible all the way back. Out to sea, rough waters mark the St Aldhelm's Head tidal race.

This is a potentially treacherous stretch of coast, which has claimed its share of shipwrecks. One of the worst was during a wild night in January 1786, when an East indiaman with 242 people on board, the *Halsewell*, was wrecked near Seacombe. One of the crew managed to clamber up the cliffs to sound the alarm, and local quarrymen helped with the rescue, but 166 men and women lost their lives.

As St Aldhelm's Head is approached, the path leaves the sea-edge and begins to climb. After a few more minutes, the roof of the small chapel comes into sight. The path swings round past the stylish sculpture recalling Worth's role in the development of radar during the Second World War to reach the National Coastwatch lookout, looking a little precarious on the cliff edge. The coast path continues beyond the coastwatch station, but it is worth walking the very short distance inland to visit the Norman chapel.

The isolated chapel of St Aldhelm is a remarkable building, dating back to the late twelfth century. Its square shape is unusual for a religious building: it is believed to have served as a chantry, where priests performed masses for the safety of seafarers. A local story has it that the chapel was erected by a father who had watched helplessly as his newly-married daughter and her bridegroom were drowned just off the headland. It seems quite possible that, at one time, the roof held a beacon to warn others at sea of the dangers of this stretch of coast.

The chapel began to fall into disrepair, and was only restored as a chapel in the nineteenth century. However, the carved dates on the central pillar – including 1629, 1665 and several sets of initials – are thought to be genuine. A superstition which continued well into living memory had it that it was lucky to make a wish while dropping a pin into one of the holes in this pillar. The chapel is still used for occasional church services.

Continue from St Aldhelm's Head along the coast path. As the path turns the corner of the headland, a fine view along the coast towards Portland comes into sight. The impressive white cliff in the distance is at Worbarrow, where the chalk Purbeck hills drop into the sea. A little nearer, providing an obvious geological contrast, is the ragged limestone edge of Gad Cliff, also inside the Army ranges. Coming back along the coast from Gad the low shaley cliffs of Kimmeridge, with the thin finger of the Clavell Tower, can be seen, as can the high land of Swyre Head and nearer still Houns Tout Cliff.

The path drops sharply, and then immediately climbs again. This is a stiff climb, which deserves to be taken gently. From the top, continue along the edge of the cliff, beside a large pasture. In due course, the semi-circle of Chapman's Pool comes into sight directly below the path. A few wooden boathouses can also been seen at the water's edge.

Cross a stile by a war memorial into a grassy hillside, which slopes down on your left towards the sea. Keep the stone wall to your right, and carry on until Chapman's Pool is behind you, and a small stone waymarking stone is reached. (This is the place to double back down the hill if you want to visit Chapman's Pool itself; Walk 10 will also take you to Chapman's Pool.)

At the stone turn right, cross the stile, and follow a track through the two fields emerging at a stile on to the road to St Aldhelm's Head. Cross the road and immediately find another path, running onwards on the left edge of a field. You will emerge shortly beside a farmyard; turn half-left, and then right to follow the tarmac road back to Worth village.

7. THE STORY OF STONE

Langton Matravers – Acton – Quarr Farm – Langton Matravers

A little under 5 miles (8 kms) of country walking, exploring the heart of Purbeck's stone quarrying industry. Allow 2-3 hours.

STARTING POINT
Langton Matravers church (park nearby). Buses run from Swanage, Corfe and Wareham.

FACILITIES
The walk begins and ends close to the Kings Arms pub and Langton shop. Toilets in Langton.

ANY PROBLEMS?
Can be muddy in parts.

ABOUT THIS WALK

There's nothing dramatically beautiful about Langton Matravers in the way that perhaps there is about some of the other Purbeck stone villages – Worth or Kimmeridge, for example. Langton is strung out, as its name suggests, along a busy road from Swanage and for many visitors this is all they see as they pass through on the way to somewhere else.

This is a shame: Langton has an interesting history. Its economy has been – and to an extent still is today – focused on the quarrying industry, as the village museum (complete with a reconstruction of life underground in a old stone mine) makes amply clear. It's worth taking time, on foot, to explore the lanes which run off from the main road, particularly on the north side of the village.

Like Langton itself, there's nothing spectacular about this walk: no wildly dramatic cliff paths or sea views, for instance. There are, however, other pleasures to be had. This is the walk for anyone interested in Purbeck's stone trade, with the opportunity to inspect at close quarters a restored family quarry.

The walk will also be enjoyed by anyone who likes rediscovering the old green lanes of England: the half-forgotten routes which could have become busy tarmac roads if history had been different. Instead the lanes, now merely farm tracks, footpaths or bridleways, serve as a reminder of how all country roads used to be.

THE WALK

Walk down Langton's main street from the church, passing the Kings Arms. Turn right into The Hyde. Just past the last of the houses, before the road becomes a private drive, turn left up a little path. Almost immediately, at a stile, head half-right through a gate across a small field, making for the far corner. Here, at another stile, follow a farm track. It swings left across a field, making for a gateway in the further corner of the field.

Beyond this gateway, the track continues as a pleasant lane, shortly with dry-stone walls to both left and right. After a few hundred metres, the lane arrives at a junction. Turn right here on to the Priests Way.

The Priests Way can be followed all the way between Swanage and Worth Matravers. Many centuries ago, Swanage's church was only a daughter chapel to the main church at Worth, and this was the path, so it is said, that the Worth priests took as they walked across to Swanage for their pastoral duties.

Follow the Priests Way, a quiet lane at this point running between stone walls. It shortly bends to the right, skirting Spyway Barn over to your left. Continue (you will pass footpaths leaving right to Tom's Field and Langton and left to Dancing Ledge), until you approach an active quarrying area. At a gate and stile, turn right – the houses of Acton are now directly ahead of you.

Approaching Acton, take the right-hand walled track and pass the first houses. Look for a very narrow path on your right at the back of Highland Cottages. Take this path, and continue as it becomes a track, bending round to the left past the houses.

Acton is a fascinating settlement, built for the quarrymen and their families from stone taken straight from the neighbouring fields.

On reaching a tarmac road turn right, but almost immediately (just past the last house) turn right on to a field footpath which heads off

diagonally across a sizeable field. Cross the main Langton/Kingston road and take the track opposite towards a row of houses.

Don't miss the opportunity to take a look at the restored stone quarry on the right, at the end of the track. The National Trust has cleared away the undergrowth which invaded Norman's Quarry when it became disused, so that it is now possible to see the quarry buildings, the remains of the capstan and the sloping tunnel itself to the quarry face. This is a valuable reminder of the way that a traditional small family stone quarry was operated, aided by the horse or donkey which slowly circled around with the capstan to haul up the stone.

At the track end, choose the footpath half-left which runs diagonally across the large field before you. The line of the path should be easy to follow, as a dark green streak in the grass. Make for the far corner of Langton West Wood. At this point, turn right, taking the path which initially runs alongside the western edge of the wood. Pass from the first field through a gate into a second and then make for the stile ahead, to head for the large green barn at Quarr Farm.

Quarr Farm ('quarry' in local dialect) is today very obviously a place of work. The house, just visible behind the other farm buildings, dates from the eighteenth century, though parts of an earlier seventeenth century house are incorporated into it.

The area near here was for generations the area where Purbeck 'marble' was quarried. The marble, a particularly hard intractable limestone, outcrops only in a narrow band along the hillside. The Romans quarried it near Wilkswood. Later, in mediaeval times, considerable quantities of Purbeck marble were required for many of the great cathedrals, including Salisbury Cathedral and Westminster Abbey. Anyone who has tested the hardness of this stone can only have tremendous admiration for the skills of the mediaeval masons who shaped and carved it with such apparent ease. The marble was

The Priests Way

taken to Corfe Castle where some of the working of the stone took place, before being transported across the heath to Ower on the edge of Poole Harbour for loading on to boats.

Skirt round the green barn and follow the bridleway sign through a gate into the woodland, past a welcoming National Trust sign. This is one of the most pleasant sections of the walk, and it's easy to stride out through the wood and miss the next turn. Look out for a path crossing (a stile away to your left confirms that this is the place), and here turn right. The path drops down the hillside, emerging out of the wood into a field beyond. The line of the path can be clearly followed from here, bending in due course to meet the left side of the field at a gate. Cross through into the next field, but immediately turn right to continue alongside the field boundary. At the top leave through a metal gate, cross a small field and emerge on to a track by a farmyard.

Take the track, but turn left at the first house (Durnford View) and keep ahead initially on a little road and then a path before emerging at the edge of a large field. Carry straight ahead, keeping the stone wall to your right. Just before the wall bends out, find a stile into a tiny passageway to your right. This takes you back, beside Langton churchyard, to the starting point for the walk.

8. AROUND CORFE CASTLE

Corfe Castle – Corfe Common – Little Woolgarston – Challow Hill – Corfe Castle

A attractive 4 mile (6.5 km) exploration of some of the countryside immediately adjacent to Corfe Castle village, including Corfe Common and a ridge section of the Purbeck Hills.

STARTING POINT
Corfe Castle village, by the church. Park in the West Street car park (signs from market place) or in the castle car park. Corfe is on the main Wareham-Swanage bus route, and is served by the Swanage Railway.

FACILITIES
Corfe Castle offers shops, pubs, cafes (including National Trust tea-rooms overlooking the castle); public toilets.

ANY PROBLEMS?
Generally straightforward. The final descent from Challow Hill to Corfe village is steep, though steps have been provided to help.

ABOUT THIS WALK

'If one wanted to show a foreigner England, perhaps the wisest course would be to take him to the final section of the Purbeck Hills, and stand him on their summit, a few miles to the east of Corfe', wrote E.M. Forster in his novel *Howard's End*. Forster duly arranged for one of his characters, Frieda Liesecke, to be escorted here, to gaze down over the Dorset heathland, the waters of Poole Harbour, and the distant lands beyond.

Quite where on the Corfe ridge fictional Frieda was taken isn't clear,

Corfe Castle

WALK 8 • AROUND CORFE CASTLE

but I would have recommended that she headed for Challow Hill, the hill directly to the east of Corfe Castle itself. Challow Hill offers a full panorama, not just down towards Poole Harbour but also south, across to the villages of Kingston and Langton, and westwards, where the line of the Purbeck ridge of chalk hills bends round towards the English Channel. Much nearer at hand is an even more striking view, because from Challow Hill it's possible to look *down* into the very heart of Corfe's castle.

You'll reach Challow Hill towards the end of this walk. First, though, is a very different landscape to enjoy, that of the National Trust's Corfe Common.

THE WALK

Leave Corfe's market square along West Street, passing the churchyard.

Not surprisingly, Corfe was for many centuries the most important town in Purbeck, sending members to Parliament. If you want to visualise the castle and village as they were at the time of the Civil War, the model village offers a scaled-down reconstruction. The museum underneath the old Town Hall is packed with local relics, including dinosaur footprints.

At West Street's first bend, turn left between two cottages, to emerge at a small recreation ground. Turn right here, following the sign to Kingston and Chapman's Pool (the path to take is the one which meanders across the common land beyond the playing field, not the one which hugs the right-hand side of the field).

Continue through a gate at the far end of the field and then, almost immediately, through a kissing gate, to emerge into a second large field. Keep on the well-defined path, following the footpath signs when you reach a small housing development. Shortly after the last of the houses, you will reach Corfe Common.

Corfe Common is the largest common in Dorset. It's designated as a Site of Special Scientific Interest, the wetter areas of the common being particularly of interest for naturalists. A number of rare species of beetle and damselfly are to be found here.

Keep to the edge of the common, making a ninety-degree turn left beyond the last of the houses and gardens. Leave the common through a gate, and turn right on to a quiet street to reach the main Swanage road, just at the point where the road from Kingston comes in.

Cross the Swanage road, and immediately re-enter Corfe Common, taking the bridleway signed to Woolgarston. Keep to the track as it crosses the Swanage Railway on a small stone bridge; beyond the bridge bear right, taking the track which climbs a little rise before dropping back down to a small valley. The track climbs again, bending this time to the left and heading for a gate in the far corner at the end of the common. Once through the gate you will find yourself looking down on the cottages at Little Woolgarston.

Little Woolgarston is one of a number of settlements along the base of the Purbeck hills. One of the cottages before you, a

combination of Purbeck stone and thatch set in a wonderful garden, dates back to the eighteenth century.

Cross the field in front of the houses. Turn left, and just past the second thatched cottage take the footpath (signed Woolgarston) off to the right. Initially the path runs between a hedge and a tall fence (this section can be overgrown in high summer; if it seems too difficult, simply carry on up the Little Woolgarston lane, turning right at the end). Very soon, you cross a stile to enter a field. Climb the rise to find the stile you are aiming for. The path can be followed easily, over a number of stiles and through two fields, until you reach an unclassified tarmac road. Turn left briefly on to the road, before turning right up a waymarked bridleway which runs up towards the hills.

Turn right along the path at the base of the hill, before – after a few hundred metres – turning back sharp left on to the chalky track climbing up to the hill top. From here, follow the well-used ridgeway track to the telecommunications mast a little way ahead of you.

At the mast, make use of a concessionary footpath (not shown on the Ordnance Survey map) to keep to the hilltop, to take you on to Challow Hill. After a few minutes of walking, the ruins of the keep of Corfe Castle lie directly below. Turn left here, and take the steep path down the hillside. Turn right under the railway bridge, and then left at the main road, to reach the centre of Corfe village.

9. THE HILLS AND THE HEATH

Corfe Castle – Knowle Hill – Ridgeway Hill – Grange Arch –
Stonehill Down – Norden Wood – Corfe Castle

Fabulous walking on the Purbeck ridgeway, with a little taste of the Purbeck heathland to conclude. This 6½ mile (10.5 km) walk is not particularly strenuous and offers a great views. Allow 2½-5 hours.

STARTING POINT
Corfe Castle village. Park in the West Street car park (signs from market place) or in the castle car park. Corfe is on the main Wareham-Swanage bus route, and served by the Swanage Railway.

FACILITIES
In Corfe Castle .

ANY PROBLEMS?
Generally, fairly problem-free.

ABOUT THIS WALK

This walk, over the springy turf of the chalk downs west of Corfe and through a quiet woodland area of the heath, offers two contrasting Purbeck landscapes to enjoy.

'Landscape', we probably need to remember, is more than just a view. It's more, too, than the sort of approach that a geologist or a naturalist would take to a particular stretch of countryside, concerned just with the rocks or with the flora and fauna. It's about the way we relate as humans to an area of land, and the sorts of associations which it evokes in us.

In the case of both the chalk downs and the Purbeck heathland, human engagement over many centuries has clearly shaped both landscapes. Look down from the hill ridge as you walk and the lands below you can be read for the history they contain. You will see the places where, many hundreds of years ago, humans chose to build their farmsteads and settlements; you will see the field boundaries and enclosures with which they divided the land.

This part of Purbeck is today primarily an agricultural landscape, but it's important not to forget the industrial heritage. As mentioned below, the heathland here is effectively a former industrial landscape, recovering from the time when it was the centre of a major clay extraction industry. Don't let that put you off – you'll find this is a delightful walk.

THE WALK

From Corfe village square, take the footpath round the left side of the castle mound, leaving the N.T. tea-rooms on your right. Cross the Church Knowle road and take the bridleway signed to Cocknowle.

Stay on the bridleway for a few hundred metres. By a stone waymarker, and just before the path you're on reaches a farm gate, turn right to take the green track which climbs up the hill. Near the top, make for the gate in the fence to your left to find the ridgeway path.

This path has been created relatively recently, allowing walkers to keep to the hill brow for almost the full length of this part of the Purbeck Hills. It is not currently shown on Ordnance Survey maps.

Continue along the ridgeway, watching as the village of Church Knowle draws level below you. Once the stone memorial to Ramblers' campaigner Mary Baxter is passed, views open out to the right as well, down to Poole Harbour and the heathland. Ahead, just to the right of the main chalk ridge, is Creech Barrow.

The church in Church Knowle is dedicated to St Peter and is another of Purbeck's mediaeval churches. Much of the church as it is today dates from the late thirteenth century.

The path drops down to meet the minor road between Church Knowle and Furzebrook and then continues up again, this time the hill in question being Ridgeway Hill. Another of Purbeck's delightful manor houses, Barnston may be visible briefly over to the left. Barnston manor was built in the late thirteenth century and extended in Elizabethan times when a two-storey bay was added to the south front.

After several hundred metres of climbing, the ridgeway path does

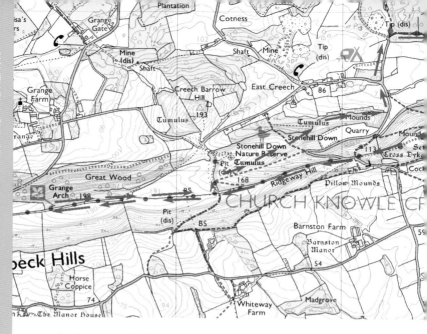

a dog-leg turn: take the gate on your left and immediately turn right to continue along the hill brow. (It's possible if you wish to shorten the walk to do so by omitting this next stretch to and from Grange Arch).

The chalk hillside here, together with the neighbouring woodland, is looked after by the Dorset Wildlife Trust. Stonehill Down is one of over forty nature reserve in the county which the Trust manages (it also has responsibility for Kilwood nature reserve on the heath just to the north-east of here).

The Trust suggests that spring and summer are the best times to appreciate Stonehill Down. Orchids (in particular the bee orchid, the early purple orchid and the common spotted orchid) can be found here in early summer, whilst downland flowers such as horseshoe vetch and rock rose attract a good variety of butterflies, including the Lulworth skipper and the Adonis blue.

Keep straight on following the ridgeway path. The English Channel is over to your left, whilst directly below is the small settlement of Steeple with its church nestling among the trees (curiously, Steeple church comes equipped with a standard church tower).

A short distance further on is the hill-top folly known as Grange Arch.

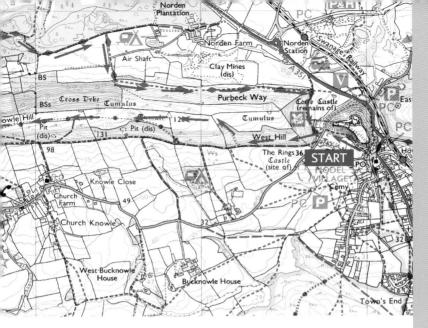

Grange Arch is also known as Bond's Folly, recollecting the name of Denis Bond who arranged for this piece of hilltop architecture to be constructed some time before the year 1746. This was a period when country landowners were taking steps to make their landscapes as 'picturesque' as possible, and Grange Arch was designed to close off the distant view from Bond's country house, Creech Grange.

Creech Grange can be seen from Grange Arch through the gap in the trees below. It is a substantial building, dating originally from the 1500s, but from this direction showing off its fine eighteenth century south front. Both Creech Grange and Tyneham House were traditionally held by branches of the Bond family.

From Grange Arch, retrace your steps until you are back at the 'dog-leg' turn. Cross back through the gate, but this time continue initially straight ahead for a few metres. The top of a deep chalk valley lies ahead; beyond, a little over to the right, is the start of a sheep track which runs diagonally up over the further hillside. This is the path to make for. Stay on it as it breasts the hill brow and continues over Stonehill Down. What began as a narrow trod gradually becomes a much more obvious footpath.

Observant map-readers will notice that, although this path is not shown as a right of way, the whole of Stonehill Down has been given

a light yellow tint. This is Ordnance Survey's way of denoting that the hillside has been designated as public access land.

The battle by walkers for open access to moors and mountains lasted over a century, eventually culminating in 2000 with the passing of the Countryside and Rights of Way Act (the CRoW Act). The so-called 'right to roam', which the Act introduced for uncultivated land, primarily transformed the opportunities for walkers in the mountains and moorlands of northern England and Wales, particularly on the grouse moors where previously 'keep out' signs had often been erected by gamekeepers. Nevertheless uncultivated downland and heathland is also included as access land under the CRoW Act.

The path you have been following heads down to meet the Furzebrook road at a gate. Turn left and continue on the road for a short distance, passing the East Creech turn and the East Creech campsite. As the road bends abruptly left, a bridleway leads off to the right. Take this path through a pleasant wood, skirting old clay workings both left and right.

East Creech from Creech Barrow Hill

It may be hard to credit, but this peaceful corner of Purbeck is an old industrial landscape. Clay had been taken from the heathland for centuries, but the industry really got going in the early nineteenth century when a London merchant Benjamin Fayle moved to the area and began to extract clay near Norden. Enterprisingly, he built an early horse-drawn plateway railway (with L-shaped rails to hold the wheels) from Norden to a wharf on Poole Harbour at Middlebere.

The second of the two great local clay companies was Pike Brothers who initially dug pits just to the north of here, at Furzebrook. What is now the Blue Pool was originally a giant clay pit operated by the firm in the first half of the nineteenth century; clay was taken to Ridge on the river Frome near Wareham, and Pike's constructed a dead-straight track across the heath to Ridge which can still be followed today. From at least the 1860s, this also became a proper narrow-gauge railway, and the tracks were later extended west to Cotness, Creech and Povington. A series of engines, named in Latin in sequence from Primus to Septimus were employed on the railway at different times.

One, Secundus, survives. For many years it was preserved on public display in Birmingham, but in 2004 it was returned to Purbeck and is intended to be one of the prize exhibits in the new Purbeck Mineral and Mining Museum being created at Norden.

Keep to the woodland track, ignoring two footpaths to your left. You will in due course arrive at a junction of paths; a footpath continues ahead, but keep to the bridleway, which turns right and crosses a little stream on two bridges. After a few minutes the path emerges at the right-hand edge of the wood, with green fields to your right, and beyond, the range of the Purbeck Hills. Keep along this path, passing yet another small clay pool to the left.

The land around here has been taken over as a nature reserve by the Amphibian and Reptile Conservation Trust, previously known as the Herpetological Conservation Trust. Herpetology is the study of reptiles; as mentioned earlier, all six of Britain's reptiles can be found on the Purbeck heathland.

Shortly beyond the small pool, turn right off the bridleway over a stile to enter a field. A footpath runs up the right side of the field, then joins a short muddy stretch of farm track, before entering another field straight ahead.

Cross this field, keeping directly ahead, making for a stile and gate at the foot of the hills. Once over this stile, turn sharp left, ignoring another better-defined path which climbs half-left up the hill.

The path continues for a considerable distance along the bottom of the hill, through rough ground invaded by bracken and scrub. It's impossible to go wrong - just carry on, keeping the boundary fence to your left, and admiring the occasional views down over the heathland to Poole Harbour. Finally the path emerges at a stile, directly below Corfe Castle. Cross the stile and continue ahead; almost immediately, turn right and follow a well-defined track back to the Corfe-Church Knowle road and to the centre of the village.

10. CHAPMAN'S POOL FROM CORFE

Corfe Castle – Kingston – Chapman's Pool – Corfe Castle

This 8 mile (13 km) takes you south from Corfe to the coast, visiting the village of Kingston on the way out. Allow 3-5 hours.

STARTING POINT
Corfe Castle village. Park in the West Street car park (signs from market place). Corfe is also on the main Wareham-Swanage bus route, and served by the Swanage Railway.

FACILITIES
There's a chance to break this walk at Kingston (Scott Arms pub).

ANY PROBLEMS?
Relatively straightforward; can be muddy. The path down to Chapman's Pool (and back up again) may be slippery in wet weather, and in very wet conditions may be worth avoiding altogether. Chapman's Pool suffers from cliff falls and erosion, so it is sometimes necessary to close or divert paths in the area; follow any instructions appropriately.

ABOUT THIS WALK

The temptation when starting a walk from Corfe is to make for the Purbeck Hills, but here's a walk to take you straight to the coast – to the small cove which is Chapman's Pool.

Kingston church is the dominant landmark on the outward leg. It is in fact the second church the village has had – the old church still stands, though it is now privately owned. It was not grand enough for the third Earl of Eldon who in the 1870s commissioned the eminent architect George Edmund Street to build a more handsome edifice. St James's has been described as a miniature cathedral, and – like the mediaeval cathedrals – much use was made in it of Purbeck marble.

An old quarry near Blashenwell Farm on Corfe Common was opened specially to provide the material.

The walk begins with architecture of a more vernacular kind – Corfe's West Street, once the main road from the village to Swanage and south Purbeck, and the centre of the mediaeval marble trade. The marble would be dragged here, before being shipped from Ower on the edge of Poole Harbour. Underneath West Street, so they say, are perhaps ten feet of stone chippings, remaining as a reminder of the huge quantity of marble and stone which was stored and worked here.

THE WALK

Walk down West Street from Corfe's market place, until the houses end and the road stops abruptly at a turning circle. Go through the gate on to Corfe Common and take the well-walked path running off half-left. Follow this path over wooden walkways across marshy ground and up to the first brow. Here turn right, and after a short distance you will arrive at a low stone block. Turn left at this point and follow a less defined path down the hillside; after a while it will swing round towards the right. At the edge of the common at the bottom, search for the kissing gate in among the trees.

Follow the path from here over a stream, across a water meadow, and into an irregularly shaped field. Follow the path diagonally across this field, picking up the edge of another field shortly. You briefly

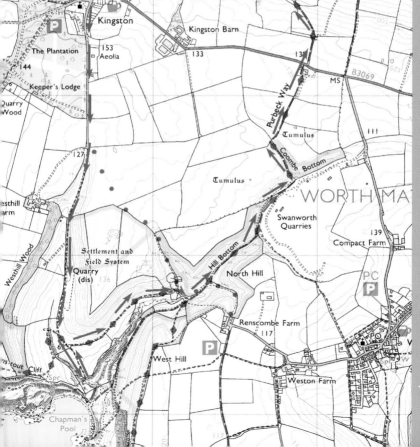

Blashenwell Farm and Corfe Castle

enter a shady lane between two fields. Keep to the left of the next two fields, passing West Lynch Farm a short distance away on your right. At the next stile, follow the path across the middle of a meadow, almost directly towards Kingston church tower.

The path now enters woodland. Turn right on to a track, and then immediately left, past a row of cottages. Turn right up old stone steps into a little alley which will take you to the centre of Kingston village.

Kingston is an estate village, the estate being that of Encombe House, a fine country house half a mile away in a secluded valley near

The Scott Arms, Kingston

the coast. The pub, the Scott Arms, records the family name: John Scott was a successful politician, who when he became Lord Chief Justice in 1799 was made the first Lord Eldon and who bought the Encombe estate in 1807 (see the introduction to Walk 11).

Long before Scott, however, Kingston really did belong to the King, or at least to the royal house of Wessex. Records report that it was given by a certain King Edred to the abbess of Shaftesbury in 948, who also acquired the 'right of wreck', the valuable right to salvage anything wrecked or washed up on the beaches nearby.

Take the minor road opposite, keeping the church to your right. The road heads almost due south, making straight for the sea. The tarmac may not be the best surface for walking, but traffic will be almost non-existent.

As you approach the coast, the road bends to the left. The coast path leaves to the right to climb up Houns Tout Cliff, but keep on the track for a short distance further, looking out for a waymark stone. Turn right here, climbing a stile to follow a field footpath to the edge of the cove. Beyond here, follow the clayey path down through the undergrowth, to reach the little rocky beach at Chapman's Pool.

Chapman's Pool is the backdrop to a classic animal story *Seal Summer,* by the author Nina Warner Hooke. The book tells the tale of the summer of 1961 when a wild grey seal arrived unexpectedly at Chapman's Pool, and (much to the delight of visitors) staying from May to November. The seal's story reached the media, who decided to give him the name of 'Sammy'. *Seal Summer* tells of Sammy's encounters with local people and holidaymakers and of the desperate attempts to prevent one family from having him shot.

Take the footpath back from Chapman's Pool to regain the main track. Continue along it past a small settlement of cottages, staying on it as it bends to the right past Hill Bottom Cottage and then bends back towards the left. At this point look for the waymark to Corfe, and turn left off the track up a green valley.

This attractive path is the southern section of the Purbeck Way, a waymarked route which begins at Wareham, takes in Corfe, and ends here at Chapman's Pool. (The final leg of Walk 9, through Norden Wood, also followed the Purbeck Way).

There's no need for detailed instructions for the next mile or so. Simply continue up the path you're on as it gradually climbs from the coast to the Langton/Kingston road.

Cross over and take the bridleway immediately opposite. Now, abruptly, the views open up; there, below, is Corfe Castle standing proud, the line of the Purbeck Hills on either side, and Poole Harbour beyond.

The bridleway gently descends, making for easy walking. Don't be lulled into complacency, however: ignore the first footpath joining from the left but, almost immediately, leave the bridleway as it bends round towards the right, taking a footpath which leaves to the left (or, more precisely, half-left).

After a very short section of lane go through a kissing gate into a field, keeping to the left-hand field boundary. Leave through another gate into a second field, and then head through a third gate into a smaller field. Leave this also by a kissing gate, cross a small bridge, and enter another field, this time following the right-hand field boundary. Pass between a cottage and its vegetable garden, to reach the edge of Corfe Common.

Head just slightly left as you enter the common, taking the most significant track. Follow this to a small concrete waymark post and at this point turn left, crossing the Kingston road again. Now take the path which heads half-right, aiming for the corner of the common by the garden of a house. Turn to walk up the edge of the common, to find a footpath back to Corfe. (This final section is the reverse of the start of Walk 8). Pass between some houses before finding the two large meadows which lie between West Street and East Street. Follow the path back to the centre of the village.

11. A BREATH OF SEA AIR

Kingston – Houns Tout – Coast Path – Swyre Head – Kingston

A 5½ mile (8.75 km) 2-4 hour walk from Kingston to the coast and back, encircling Encombe House.

STARTING POINT
Kingston. Buses run from Swanage, Corfe and Wareham. If driving, carry on through Kingston village to find the car park.

FACILITIES
Kingston's pub, the Scott Arms, provides food as well as drinks, and is popular with visitors.

ANY PROBLEMS?
The coast path can, in some weather conditions, be slippery. There is a climb up to Swyre Head. The coast path between Chapman's Pool and Kimmeridge suffers from cliff erosion and cliff falls. It may occasionally be necessary to divert or temporarily close the path.

ABOUT THIS WALK

This may very well be the breeziest walk in the book. The wind can whip along the hill-brow above Encombe House, and is always stronger once the coast itself is reached, high up on the cliff edge at Houns Tout. Good for blowing away the cobwebs, certainly; perhaps not quite so advisable on a very windy day.

The walk describes a circle around one of the most sheltered corners of Purbeck, the quiet valley of Encombe, which has sometimes been described as the 'Golden Valley'. Encombe House itself is Purbeck's most architecturally impressive country house. It lies in the landscaped parkland below for much of the walk, although there's only really one opportunity to see it clearly and that is from the top of Swyre Head. (Encombe is not regularly open to the public).
Encombe House was built about 1770, probably by the then owner

John Pitt. Architectural scholars all agree that the house is a fine achievement: 'an amateur architect has rarely produced a building as powerful as Encombe,' says John Newman in Pevsner's guide to Dorset buildings. From the house, the succession of artificial lakes to the south give the illusion that the sea actually laps at the terrace.

The Encombe estate came to John Pitt in 1734 and passed in due course to his son, William Morton Pitt, a cousin of William Pitt the Younger. William Morton Pitt was also an MP, for some thirty-six years, but was more concerned to improve the conditions of working people in Purbeck than to follow a successful career at Westminster. He campaigned against workhouses and in favour of smallholdings for local cottagers. He opened a rope factory in Kingston and developed a straw-plait industry in Langton and Corfe, with the idea of providing more local employment opportunities. He sponsored education and tried to encourage local children to read and write.

In 1807 however he sold the Encombe estate. It was purchased by John Scott, recently ennobled as Lord Eldon, a politician of a very different political tendency. Eldon was a controversial figure, determined to destroy the ripples of radicalism spreading from the French Revolution across the channel, which he did by suspending Habeas Corpus and controlling the press.

One contemporary journalist wrote that Eldon 'seems to be on his guard against everything liberal and humane'. He was hated by many, including the poet Shelley who launched a venomous attack on him and his government colleagues in the poem *The Mask of Anarchy*. Using language which today might, politely, be called intemperate, Shelley wrote:

> 'Next came Fraud, and he had on,
> Like Eldon, an ermined gown;
> His big tears, for he wept well,
> Turned to millstones as they fell;

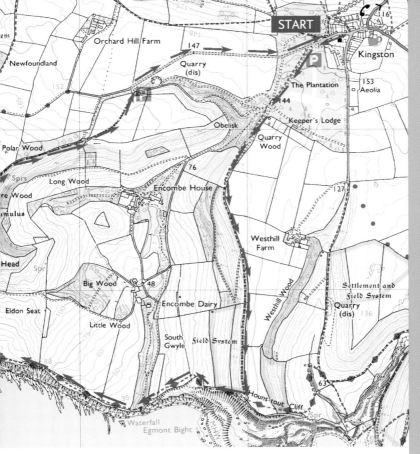

> And the little children, who,
> Round his feet played to and fro,
> Thinking every tear a gem,
> Had their brains knocked out by them.'

Eldon remained deeply conservative to his death. At the end of his life, he made the journey from Encombe to the House of Lords to speak against the 'dangerous innovation' of the Great Western Railway.

This walk provides a pleasant combination of hilltop and cliff walking, culminating at Swyre Head, the highest point in Purbeck. Altogether, therefore, this is a walk offering a great deal of interest and pleasure.

THE WALK

From the Scott Arms, walk through Kingston village past the church and cottages. Shortly afterwards, turn left along a private drive. (If using the Houns Tout car park, you will emerge directly on to this drive).

Follow the drive for a few hundred metres through a plantation. When the tarmac road bends off to the right towards Encombe House, continue almost directly ahead along a smaller path. Shortly after passing a house on your left you will arrive at a stile into a hilltop field.

The path ahead follows the brow of a steep hill. To the left is a stone wall, with views beyond to the coast. To the right the field falls down steeply to the valley where Encombe House is well hidden among the trees. Beyond, on the opposite side of the valley, is an obelisk erected in commemoration of the first Earl of Eldon's brother.

In due course the path continues into a second field, usually used as grazing land for sheep. Eventually a stile leads directly out to the coast at Houns Tout Cliff, five hundred feet (150m) above the sea below.

Houns Tout is a fine viewpoint, and a stone seat has been helpfully placed here for walkers. St Aldhelm's Head is to the left, Worbarrow Bay and Portland in the distance to the right.

Turn right, and immediately the coast path drops down quite steeply. A few hundred metres later, the path arrives at the end of the gwyle (wooded valley) which runs down to the sea from Encombe. There's a waterfall as the water from the gwyle cascades into the sea.

The coast path, however, continues up the other side of the stream. The cliffs suffer from quite serious erosion in this area and the remains of several previous generations of barbed wire fencing, marking where the coast path used to go before it slipped into the sea, can be spotted to your left in a number of places.

The path skirts the high ground of Swyre Head to the right (despite its name, Swyre Head is not on the coast), and then drops down to a bridge over a little stream. Beyond the bridge, at the first field boundary, turn right at a stile and begin to head away from the coast.

This stretch of path provides an invaluable link between Swyre Head and the coast (the next walk in this volume also uses it). The path is concessionary rather than a recognised right of way.

Egmont Bight

From the stile keep up the left-hand side of a large field. After a while, the path becomes a track. Cross two stiles and follow the path towards the foot of Swyre Head, this time following the right-hand field edge. The path begins climbing steeply up the side of the hill, but there are compensations in the fine views back to the sea and towards Smedmore House, the neighbouring country house to Encombe.

At the hilltop a stile will take you over into the grassy area surrounding Swyre Head.

The path you want is ahead, bending round to the left to head for a stone wall, but it's worth stopping briefly first at Swyre Head to admire the view. Swyre Head offers the best glimpse so far of Encombe House, down in the valley below.

The path back from Swyre Head to Kingston cuts across the grass and quickly becomes a well-worn track in the turf. Follow the wall past Polar Wood, along the opposite side of the valley from the one taken at the start of this walk. Once past the wood the track swings left, away from the brow, through the middle of a large field. The top of Kingston church can just be seen above the trees. When a tarmac road is reached after the sheep fold, turn right and follow it back to Kingston.

12. KIMMERIDGE AND SWYRE HEAD

Kimmeridge – Kimmeridge Bay – Coast Path – Swyre Head – Kimmeridge

A lovely hill walk combined with a fine stretch of the coast: altogether about 5 miles (8 kms) and taking from 2-3¾ hours.

STARTING POINT
Kimmeridge. Park in the quarry car park above the village. (The entrance is on the left, just past the junction with the Bradle/Puddle Mill by-road, before the village is reached).

FACILITIES
Kimmeridge village offers a licensed cafe. Toilets at Kimmeridge bay.

ANY PROBLEMS?
Generally, a very straightforward route. The path up to Swyre Head is something of a pull-up and can be slippery. The coast path between Chapman's Pool and Kimmeridge suffers from cliff erosion and cliff falls. It may occasionally be necessary to divert or temporarily close the path.

ABOUT THIS WALK

Geologically, the short stretch of coast near Kimmeridge Bay offers a contrast to other parts of Purbeck. In fact the technical term for the kind of rock formation found here, 'Kimmeridge clay', ensures that geologists at least know of this Purbeck village.

Peaceful today, certainly, but Kimmeridge has an interesting industrial past. As in other parts of Purbeck, human activity has tried to prise wealth from out of the earth. Here the goal has been not marble, stone or clay but the bituminous shale known as blackstone.

The story goes back a long way, to Bronze Age times, when Kimmeridge shale was fashioned into ornamental armlets. The Romans

Clavell's Tower, Kimmeridge

developed this industry, carving table-legs and other items from the shale with considerable skill.

There was another flurry of industrial activity in the seventeenth century when the local landowner Sir William Clavell launched two ultimately disastrous business ventures. His first effort, to extract alum deposits from the shale, seemed initially promising but he was up against other alum producers who claimed that they alone had authority from the Crown. Undaunted he tried again, this time developing a glassmaking works using the local blackstone as fuel. To export the glass, and salt which he was extracting from the sea, he built a large jetty which one contemporary account describes as a 'strong huge peere of Stone, 100 foote long, 50 foote highe, and 60 foote broade'. Sadly Clavell was again unlucky, getting enmeshed in litigation and being sent on two occasions to a debtor's prison, before returning to Kimmeridge to rescue his estate. His pier is reported to have been destroyed in a storm in 1745.

His bad luck seems also to have dogged numerous nineteenth century companies who also felt that the blackstone could be commercially exploited. From 1848 onwards, Kimmeridge blackstone was converted among other things into varnish, pitch, paraffin wax, dyes, and fertiliser. For a short time it was made into gas to light the streets of Paris: the problem was that it gave off a very unpleasant smell. Later, another company tried to use it in sewage purification.

It is only in the twentieth century that the wealth beneath Kimmeridge's soil was successfully tapped. Testing for oil began in the 1930s and recommenced in the 1950s. Since the late 1950s BP has operated an unobtrusive but commercially important 1800 foot (540m) oil well just to the west of Kimmeridge Bay.

None of this history, however, needs to concern you if you are simply interested in finding a peaceful and pleasant place to walk. The combination in this circular walk of the coast path from Kimmeridge Bay and the limestone ridgeway path back from Swyre Head provides enough interest by itself.

THE WALK

Leave the quarry car park, turn briefly right along the road, and immediately take the first footpath, left, which drops down the hillside to emerge at Kimmeridge churchyard below.

Walk down the main street past the houses (beyond the houses, walkers have been given a path just to the side of the road to avoid the traffic). Continue down the toll road towards the bay. As the road forks (with cars for the beach taking the right fork) continue straight ahead, and turn right immediately into a track to an upper car park. A gap in the hedge ahead leads to steps and a small bridge over a stream. You emerge close to the water's edge in a boat park.

Turn left, and pick up the coast path which climbs up the cliff towards Clavell Tower.

After decay and dereliction in the twentieth century, Clavell Tower is set for a much brighter future in the twenty-first, thanks to the recent restoration efforts of the Landmark Trust.

The tower itself has been a prominent landmark since 1830 or so, when it was erected by one of the local Clavell family, John Richards Clavell, perhaps as an observatory or perhaps simply as a folly. Later it was used for a time by coastguards; Thomas Hardy also came this way, and included a sketch of the tower when he published his *Wessex*

Poems. But by the middle of the last century the building had been gutted by fire and was becoming nothing more than a ruin.

It wasn't just the poor state of repair which threatened the tower, however, it was also the sea, which year after year was eroding the cliff on which the building stood. It was clear that, if nothing was done, the Clavell Tower would one day tumble straight down the cliff towards Kimmeridge Ledges.

The Landmark Trust, working with a small charitable trust set up locally, secured the help of the Heritage Lottery Fund and came up with plans to take down the tower and rebuild it about twenty-five metres inland. Each of the 16,000 stones or so from the old building was numbered and then reassembled on the new site, with about 300 new carved stones added to return the tower as close as possible to its original appearance. Clavell Tower is now in the safekeeping of the Landmark Trust and is used as holiday accommodation (it takes 2 people). Be warned, what must be one of the most romantic holiday lets in Purbeck seems to be solidly booked up many months in advance.

Pass the circular foundation where the tower used to stand and continue on the coast path, enjoying the views of St Aldhelm's Head and its chapel more or less straight ahead.

The path turns a corner at Rope Lake Head (St Aldhelm's now appears over on the right-hand side). Look out now for the footpath leaving the coast path to climb to Swyre Head (this path may already be familiar to you: it features in Walk 11). After crossing the stile, keep to the path up the left-hand side of a field; cross two stiles, and continue, this time following the right-hand field edge. Scramble up the hillside, to arrive at Swyre Head itself.

Swyre Head, 666 feet high (203m), beats the Purbeck Hills in height by about ten feet.

Turn left, pass the trig point stone, and take the pleasant track which runs along the limestone ridge. This is delightful walking; the Purbeck Hills are close at hand to your right, whilst down to your left you will see Smedmore House.

Smedmore is another of Purbeck's country houses, dating back to the seventeenth century, though much changed in the middle of the eighteenth century. It's a pleasant place with lovely gardens which are occasionally open to the public.

The Smedmore estate lands have not been put up for sale since 1391, when the Clavell family first acquired them. There has, however, been at least one occasion when the future of the estate was in doubt. When Rev John Clavell died in 1833, no will could be found. Under the laws of intestacy Smedmore was all set to pass to his nearest relative, his niece Louisa, and her husband Col John Mansel, when three months after the death the clergyman's former housekeeper unexpectedly produced a will apparently leaving the property to a neighbouring farmer. The lawyers were brought in, and eventually a jury at Dorchester found in favour of the niece's claim and against the will.

Continue on the ridge track which eventually begins to drop down to meet the tarmac road from Bradle to Kimmeridge, Turn left and you will find the quarry car park a very short distance beyond.

13. BY GAD – KIMMERIDGE TO TYNEHAM

Kimmeridge – Gad Cliff – Worbarrow – Tyneham – Kimmeridge Bay – Kimmeridge

A superb 7½ mile (12 km) walk from Kimmeridge along the beautiful hill-ridge to Worbarrow and the lost village of Tyneham. Surely one of the finest coastal walks in the country. Allow 2½-5 hours.

This walk is across the Lulworth Army Ranges, and access is not always possible. Check the information boards (at various places, including Lulworth, Stoborough and Corfe), search online or telephone 01929 404819. The footpaths are usually open at weekends, on public holidays and daily throughout August.

STARTING POINT
Kimmeridge: park in the quarry car park above the village. (The entrance is on the left, just past the junction with the Bradle/Puddle Mill by-road, before the village is reached; Walk 12 also begins from this car park).

FACILITIES
Toilets in Tyneham. Licensed cafe in Kimmeridge village.

ANY PROBLEMS?
Very well-marked paths, especially on the Army Ranges. Quite a lot of up and down, including the climb out of Tyneham village back to Gad Cliff.

ABOUT THIS WALK

'To those who never visited the valley I cannot hope to convey its atmosphere and spirit which were unique and gave to Tyneham its peculiar fascination.

   'Descriptions of the ancient house and the surrounding country may indeed bring back to those who loved them something of their

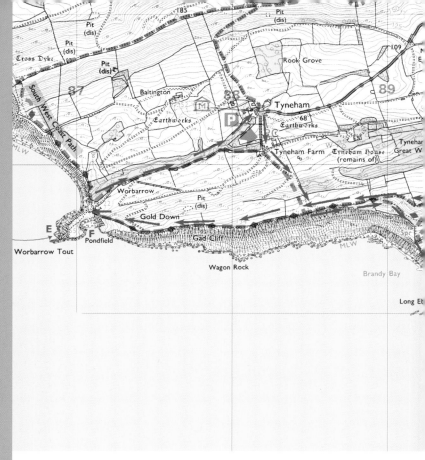

quiet, compelling charm, but its quality is inexpressible in words and that elusive quality was the essential Tyneham.'

So begins *Tyneham: A Lost Heritage*, Lilian Bond's powerful and evocative account of family and village life in Tyneham in the early years of the last century, written by a member of the family whose roots in Tyneham went back to 1683, the year when Mrs Bond's ancestor Nathaniel Bond first purchased the Elizabethan house and estate.

Lilian Bond's book is of general interest to anyone interested in social and rural history but it has a special poignancy, given that its subject-matter is a village and a way of life which disappeared abruptly and by official decree, in a particularly dramatic fashion.

Tyneham: A Lost Heritage was first published in 1956 and already, as the paragraphs quoted above make clear, Lilian Bond is writing in

the past tense. The story of the Army take-over of the village during
the last war is widely known; it was in December 1943, just before
Christmas, that the Army requisitioned all the land and houses of the
village and evacuated the local people. The land was needed according
to the Army to extend the nearby Lulworth firing ranges, and would be
held for the 'duration of the emergency'.

When they left, the villagers pinned a modest notice to the church
door: 'Please treat the church and houses with care; we have given up
our homes where many of us lived for generations to help win the war
to keep men free. We shall return one day and thank you for treating
the village kindly'.

Other parts of Purbeck, especially the heathlands bordering Poole
Harbour, were taken over by the Army during the war years and
then given back once peace had returned. But the Army's red flags

remained flying over Tyneham. In 1948, the former residents learned that the land was to be compulsorily purchased – and despite angry local allegations of broken promises and a public enquiry the sale went ahead.

The houses at Tyneham and Worbarrow, including Tyneham House and the church, were boarded up and began to disintegrate. As a child I was taken on a number of occasions to visit Tyneham, on those weekend and holiday days when the Army opened the gates on the range and allowed motorists to drive down. It was an intensely depressing place. The cottages, half tumbled down, were completely overgrown and securely fenced off. Signs warned of unexploded shells. The church, or what could be seen of it, was out-of-bounds and although the track to Worbarrow was opened it was impossible to explore the countryside or walk along the coast path.

Tyneham House, a listed building, was also out-of-bounds, and (hidden in Tyneham Great Wood) conveniently out of sight as well. Most of the house was Elizabethan, though the south-west wing dated back to mediaeval times. In 1967 the Army decided to demolish it. A few bits and pieces were taken to the County Museum or other country houses but the demolition lorries took away the rest, leaving only the mediaeval old house which survives (still out of public gaze) in a very poor condition.

Tyneham School

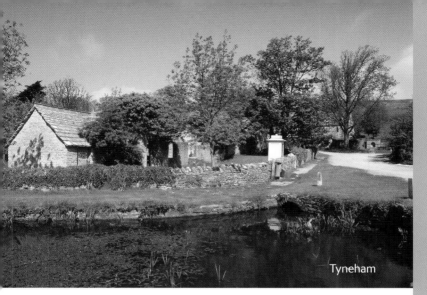
Tyneham

The destruction of Tyneham House, which many local people felt was wanton vandalism, and the continuing Army occupation of the area led to an upsurge of local protests and a vigorous campaign was begun by the Tyneham Action Group. For a time, especially when a Royal Commission recommended that the lands should be given up, it seemed that the red flags might come down for good, perhaps to be replaced by National Trust signs.

In the end the Army remained but a compromise deal was struck. Public access was allowed much more frequently and the range walks were opened. The buildings in Tyneham village were spruced up and the brambles and ivy removed from the churchyard. And so it is today: the ruins are immaculately tidy, the church and village school are open again for visitors, and the Army's warning signs more discreet. But the cosmetic tidying can't replace a more fundamental sadness about the way the story has ended.

In the 1950s and 1960s, despite the destruction and the barbed wire, it still seemed possible that the village might some day live again. Today the loss of Tyneham as a living community is irrevocable, and what we have is a museum. I would almost rather, I think, still have the brambles and the dereliction.

But undertake this walk and decide for yourself. The area around Tyneham and Worbarrow has some of the finest and most spectacular scenery in southern England.

THE WALK

Leave the quarry car park, and turn right. Pass the footpath, left, down to Kimmeridge village, but take the next footpath on the left, about twenty metres beyond the road junction. The path hugs the brow of the hill, running ahead along the left-hand edge of a large field; there are fine views down to Kimmeridge village directly below and the bay, while to the right the Purbeck Hills are running parallel, also heading for Worbarrow.

The path enters a second field and the stone tower of Steeple Church (one of Purbeck's most isolated churches) comes into sight, just a little way back, on the right. A flagpole and gate announces the start of the Army land, and the path continues along the brow,

Worbarrow Bay

climbing slightly, and now following a wall to the right. Although as the signs remind us this is an Army firing range this stretch of path is at the periphery of the occupied land and farmers are able to lease land from the Army for arable farming and pasture.

Keep along the brow until the cliffs of Worbarrow Bay and of Gad come into sight; across the valley, you may notice the cars parked at the viewpoint on Whiteways Hill. Keep the wall on your right, and follow the yellow waymarks. As the coast path comes in on your left, you arrive at a well-positioned stone seat at a small clump of trees.

This is the Ocean Seat described by Lilian Bond in her book, one of her favourite places when she was a child in Tyneham House. The wall which the path has been following since entering the ranges was the boundary between the Tyneham and South Tyneham (Egliston) estates, both mentioned in the Domesday Book. Many ancient boundaries survive in the field patterns in southern Purbeck.

Pass Ocean Seat, to walk along the edge of Gad Cliff. Tyneham village lies below (a footpath runs off to the right shortly), with the church clearly visible.

Carry on along the edge of Gad Cliff, taking care at the places where the path runs close to the edge. Gad is over four hundred feet (more than 130m) high, and sheer. Hunting was stopped in Tyneham after a number of wily foxes had lured fox-hounds over the cliff edge.

The path drops gradually, and as you approach Worbarrow you're rewarded with a fine view down to the tout and the little cove of Pondfield. The white chalky cliff of Worbarrow opposite marks the arrival of the Purbeck Hills once more at the coast, twelve or more miles west of Ballard Down.

At the base of Worbarrow Tout turn right and follow the dusty track up the valley to Tyneham, perhaps the least attractive part of the walk. (Even before the war this was a necessary walk for any visitor wanting to get to the sea: cars then, as now, were left at Tyneham.)

As you arrive at Tyneham the path back is on the right, climbing up the hillside back to Gad Cliff. However, if you have time, you may want to turn left to explore what remains of the village.

Near the new public conveniences are the buildings of what was Tyneham Farm, now in relatively good condition again. Lilian Bond describes how the celebrated Dorset Blue Vinney cheese used to be made in the top floor of the dairy house. Rows of the cheese, at different stages of the ripening process, would be stood on well-scrubbed boards. According to Mrs Bond, the smell of the cheese lingered on for years after cheese-making stopped.

From Tyneham take the footpath up the hillside to Gad Cliff and Tyneham Cap, to rejoin the coast path. At one point, you may just be able to get a glimpse of the ruins of Tyneham House, further up the valley from Tyneham Farm and in among the trees of Tyneham Great Wood.

Turn left at the top of the hill, and retrace your steps to the Ocean Seat.

From the seat, leave the brow and take the coast path down the hill, heading for Kimmeridge Bay. The path drops steadily: follow the yellow waymarks, for the path may be rerouted slightly to avoid excessive erosion of the turf.

Kimmeridge Bay lies ahead, but first the path skirts the edges of two smaller bays, Brandy Bay and Hobarrow Bay. The ruins of the farm at South Egliston and of Stickland's Cottage peer out from trees which mark the wooded valley of Egliston Gwyle. The coast path continues, becoming almost a track. Carry on, until the flagpole and metal gate marks once again the Ranges boundary. Almost immediately you'll arrive at the BP pumping station.

An information board helpfully recounts some of the history of oil exploitation in Kimmeridge. An exploratory bore-hole was sunk in 1936, but it was not until the late 1950s that the geologists returned. The pumping jack (or nodding donkey) brings up crude oil from 1790 feet (537m) below the cliffs, and the oil is then taken away by road. Ultimately, with oil from the Wytch Farm field, it is transported by underground pipeline to a refinery at Hamble on Southampton Water.

Follow the path to the right of the pumping station, until you emerge on the tarmac road, a short distance from the Gaulter Gap row of cottages. Keep to the road as it bends round behind the cottages (the coast path continues on at this point, to Kimmeridge beach). Just before the road reaches a gate, by a bridge over a little stream, turn left to follow a field path back towards Kimmeridge village.

Follow the footpath towards the remains of a stone barn (now basically a pile of stones), with the little stream to your right. At the barn the path bends round into another field, still alongside the stream. Leave this field to enter a larger field, again following the right hand edge. At the far corner of this field turn right over a stile and a wooden bridge. The houses of Kimmeridge village are now very near. Follow the path, entering the left-hand side of a small field. At the end of the field you emerge into Kimmeridge's main street.

Walk up the road past a lovely collection of thatched stone cottages to the church. As the road bends round to the right, continue straight ahead walking up a flagged stone path beside the churchyard and through the field above it to make your way back to the quarry car park.

14. THE LOST WORLD OF TYNEHAM AND WORBARROW

Lulworth Cove – Arish Mell – Flowers Barrow – Tyneham – Worbarrow – Arish Mell – Radar Hill – Lulworth Cove

A tough but rewarding 9¼ mile (15 km) hike along one of the finest stretches of the Dorset coastline, taking 3½-6 hours. Worbarrow is a magnificent bay, while the ruins of Tyneham village, occupied by the Army during the last war and not returned subsequently, are still poignant.

This walk is across the Lulworth Army Ranges, and access is not always possible. Check the information boards (at various places, including Lulworth, Stoborough and Corfe), search online or telephone Ô1929 404819. The footpaths are usually open at weekends, on public holidays and daily throughout August.

STARTING POINT
Lulworth Cove. Large car park at Lulworth Cove itself (charge). Occasional buses from Dorchester and Wool station. Alternatively, the walk can be undertaken from Tyneham.

FACILITIES
As befits a popular tourist centre, Lulworth Cove is well stocked with restaurants and cafes, and a pub. Toilets. Tyneham village is equipped with toilets; no refreshments.

ANY PROBLEMS
The Army is anxious to ensure that the public does not wander off the designated paths, and the waymarking is suitably efficient. You won't get lost. But be warned: the four substantial climbs to be tackled make this the most physically demanding as well as the longest of all the walks in this book.

In certain conditions of tides it may not be safe to begin this walk on Lulworth Cove beach, in which case either divert around the top of the cove or wait for another day.

ABOUT THIS WALK

It is in the west that geography lets down Purbeck's claim of being an island. To the south and east Purbeck is bounded by the English Channel, and anyone entering Purbeck from the north over the River Frome at Wareham does at least have to cross water of some kind. But in the west only the tiny heathland stream of Luckford Lake makes any kind of natural boundary - and Luckford Lake itself peters out on the Army ranges somewhere north of Whiteway Hill.

Since the war, however, the Army firing ranges have provided a much more obvious western boundary to Purbeck than anything nature could provide. Particularly out of the summer tourist season, when the range walks and the hill road from Steeple to Lulworth are closed to the public, the villages of Kimmeridge, Creech and Church Knowle are very effectively isolated from the rest of Dorset beyond.

Even if, by this definition, this walk begins outside of the Isle of Purbeck proper it deserves its place. Lulworth Cove is well known: a small, almost circular bay, which has been popular with visitors for many years (John Keats visited it in 1820, and a local legend has it that Napoleon himself once landed here one dark night, perhaps to reconnoitre a suitable invasion site for his troops).

In summer Lulworth Cove is busy: too many cars and coaches for the narrow Dorset lanes. When the Ranges Walks are open, however, you will quickly be able to leave the crowds behind. There is spectacular coast scenery to be enjoyed as well as the particular interests of the Fossil Forest, just inside the Army Ranges, and of the

The Fossil Forest

Iron Age hill-fort at Flowers Barrow. There is also public access, when the Walks are open, to two rocky bays at Mupe and Worbarrow.

There is no access, however, to the little cove of Arish Mell, once a remote and unspoilt corner of the Dorset coast as attractive as its name. T.E. Lawrence (Lawrence of Arabia) who lived the last years of his life in Clouds Hill Cottage on the heath north of Bovington used to swim there with friends. The little beach was apparently well-known for its brightly coloured pebbles, which according to one account were collected by local men and women, sorted by hand and then run up the beach in wheelbarrows to be taken away by lorries to end their life at local pottery works as decorations on ornamental vases and bowls.

Poor Arish Mell. It is now one of the saddest places in Purbeck. The coast path passes it by, with the beach out-of-bounds behind a wire fence and a locked gate. Arish Mell has suffered twice over – not just from the effects of Army firing practice but also from an invisible and more insidious danger. When the atomic research station was built on the heath at Winfrith in the late 1950s, a pipeline carrying waste from the experimental heavy water reactor was laid across the Ranges to Arish Mell, where the waste could be discharged into the sea from an outfall on the beach.

Nevertheless, don't let Arish Mell's plight put you off undertaking this walk. For years this area was closed to the public: I suggest you

make the most of the limited concession we have now been given to see this beautiful stretch of the coastline for yourself.

THE WALK

The walk begins on the beach itself at Lulworth Cove. Turn left on to the beach, and walk about two-thirds of the way along the cove, picking your way over the pebbles. Pass a flight of wooden steps disappearing up from the beach, and almost immediately take a path climbing diagonally up from the cove to a memorial stone on the clifftop. At this stone turn left, and you will quickly reach the fence which marks the edge of the Army ranges.

Go through the metal gate in the fence (it will be firmly locked if the Range Walks are closed). The path along the cliff edge lies ahead, clearly bounded on both sides by yellow markers.

It is possible to turn right immediately after entering the ranges to view the 'Fossil Forest'. The strange lobster-pot shaped fossils are the remains not of trees but of the algae which built up around the trunks of trees some twenty million years ago. The trees themselves are gone, represented just by the holes in the centre of the fossilised remains.

Even if you choose not to make the diversion, some of the

fossilised stumps can be clearly seen from the cliff path after another few hundred metres, looking like curious cylindrical rocks.

Ahead lies the Purbeck coast: to the right, St Aldhelm's Head closes the view in the distance, while Houns Tout, Swyre Head and the Clavell Tower at Kimmeridge are all visible, and the jagged edge of Gad Cliff also soon comes into sight. The path turns to skirt an inlet, and shortly afterwards some steps lead down to the rocky beach of Mupe Bay.

The path turns along the top of Mupe Bay, and now begins a tough climb up the side of Bindon Hill. At the top turn right to continue on the coast path. The climb is worth it for the view, which includes the waters of Poole Harbour in the distance and the range of Purbeck Hills stretching round towards Swanage.

The path continues gently downhill along a narrow ridge. The cliff edge is directly to the right, while to the left the hill falls sharply to a plain, criss-crossed by the tracks of tanks. Finally the path descends to Arish Mell.

There's another steep climb up from Arish Mell until at last the first of the ramparts of Flowers Barrow are reached. Although a large part of this Iron Age hill-fort has fallen into the sea, what is left is still impressive. The path runs through the earth ramparts until the heart of the fort is reached.

Lulworth Cove

Flowers Barrow occupies a breathtaking position, on the edge of the cliffs rising to 565 feet (170m) above sea-level. It is one of a number of hill-forts in this part of Dorset – Maiden Castle near Dorchester being the most famous – which are assumed to have been centres of power for the Durotriges, the Celtic people who lived in this area in the years before the Roman invasion, and who have given modern-day Dorset its name. It seems probable that Flowers Barrow was stormed by Vespasian's Second Legion in the years after AD43.

Flowers Barrow is associated with Purbeck's best-known ghost story, of a phantom army which was seen marching from here along the crest of the Purbeck Hills towards Creech in the year 1678. At the time the army seemed only too real to local people: over 100 people are reported to have seen it, and to have heard 'a great clashing of arms'. Among them was the local landowner of Creech Grange, John Lawrence. He and his brother immediately rushed to London to inform the government. A militia three hundred strong marched to Wareham and the bridge was barricaded but all for no purpose . . . The army vanished.

At Flowers Barrow the coast path turns off to the right; however, our path carries straight ahead, on the ridgeway of what is the final section of the Purbeck Hills. This is a delightful hilltop walk, again with views ahead towards Poole Harbour and the heathland. The path continues past a triangulation stone and then drops down towards the road from Creech to Lulworth. Just before the road is reached turn sharp right and cut back down the side of the hill along a dusty track. Tyneham church and the remains of the village are below you. (See introduction to Walk 13 for more about Tyneham).

Pass Tyneham church and at the car parking area turn right across the picnic area to find the woodland walk which has been constructed through beautiful Tyneham Gwyle. At the end of the woodland walk, turn right to take the track down to Worbarrow. The edge of Gad Cliff is above you to the left and on fine days the Isle of Portland is visible directly ahead. Once at Worbarrow drop down towards the beach and pick up the waymarks for the coast path.

Worbarrow remains attractive even though the old fishermen's cottages are now just ruins. New plaques, erected by the County Council's Heritage Coast venture, try to set the scene but it is hard to imagine the pre-war bustle that took place when mackerel shoaled in the Bay:

'When a quantity of mackerel were secured in the net the sight was one to be remembered. The fish lay quiet until they had almost reached the shore. Then all at once the water churned and broke in a hundred places simultaneously and fish leapt high into the air, their curved wet bodies glittering with all the colours of the rainbow as they flashed into the sunlight and fell back again into the seething mass below. Women ran knee deep into the waves to help support the weight of mackerel in the straining net and slowly, inch by inch, the heavy catch was dragged out of the sea and up the shelving shore.

'The moment that the shoal was seen to be enclosed a telegram had left the coastguard station and very soon the dealers' carts arrived from Wareham. The fish were counted, packed into boxes and sent off to inland markets still alive and dripping from the sea'. (*Tyneham*, Lilian Bond).

The path continues along the edge of Worbarrow Bay, beginning to climb up the side of the chalk downs. This is yet another steep clamber, to take us back once again to Flowers Barrow.

From Flowers Barrow follow the path back to Arish Mell, and then climb up the hill beyond until the top of Bindon Hill is reached.

Over to the right, Lulworth Castle can be seen among the trees. From the coast path it appears to be a real fortified mediaeval castle, but appearances are deceptive. It was built in the early seventeenth

Jousting, Lulworth Castle

century as a country house, and the castle fortifications are merely an architectural whim. The castle was completely gutted in a fire in 1929, but it is now restored.

The Weld family, the local landowners, allowed a group of Trappist monks from France to live nearby during the Napoleonic period and their presence is still commemorated by the name Monastery Farm on current maps.

At the marker on Bindon Hill, this time keep straight ahead along the brow of the hill. The track becomes chalky and dusty. Pass the radar station (the hill itself is called Radar Hill), staying on the brow of the hill. Very shortly you reach the boundary fence of the Army ranges once again. Ignore the footpaths to left and right, and keep ahead walking across the turf making for a gap in an earthwork boundary.

This last stretch across the turf is a delight. The path drops down, swinging to the left. Cross a well-marked track and follow a sheep path for a short way. Shortly, over to the right, you will be able to see a small stile into a wood. Strike off to this stile and then follow the path down through the woods. You'll emerge at some steps directly above Lulworth Cove.

15. THE BACKWATERS OF POOLE HARBOUR

Arne – Shipstal Point – Arne

A final gentle 1-2½ hour walk across heathland to the peaceful waters of Poole Harbour. This 2½ mile (4 km) walk makes use of nature trails and footpaths created by the Royal Society for the Protection of Birds, who own an extensive nature reserve in the area.

STARTING POINT
Arne village. Arne is a small isolated village on the edge of the heathland; roads lead to it from Norden, near Corfe Castle, and Stoborough near Wareham. Park in the RSPB car park on the edge of the village (charge for non-members). No public transport.

FACILITIES
Toilets attached to the car park. A toy museum, with cafe, is open in Arne during the holiday season.

ANY PROBLEMS?
None! (The route includes RSPB footpaths which are not rights of way, and which will not be shown on your Ordnance Survey map.)

ABOUT THIS WALK

There's nothing at all arduous about this final walk, a little bonus at the end of the book as a reward for previous exertions. The walk leads you across the Arne nature reserve to one of the most peaceful corners of Poole Harbour.

It was mainly because the heathland around Arne provided one of the very few breeding habitats for the Dartford Warbler that the RSPB first acquired a reserve in this area. The very cold winter of 1962-3 almost entirely wiped out the bird, and there were reported to be less than a dozen pairs in Britain in 1964. Fortunately, numbers

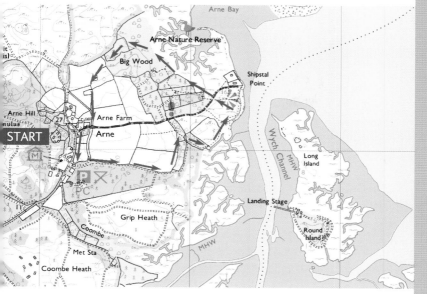

have increased significantly since then, not only in Purbeck but also elsewhere in Dorset, in other parts of the south and south-west of England and also in East Anglia (though not yet, it would appear, anywhere very close to Dartford).

The Arne reserve offers more than just a habitat for Dartford Warblers, however. Another uncommon species here is the secretive nightjar, which you are more likely to hear than see. On the harbour little egrets are a common sight especially in the autumn, whilst winter brings peak numbers of avocets to the reserve. Migrating ospreys put down in the harbour in autumn, too.

Perhaps less immediately attractive to non-naturalists is another creature of the Arne heathland, the Purbeck mason wasp, a very rare red, black and yellow insect which lives in only a handful of heathland sites around Poole. (Don't kill it.)

The RSPB took over the Arne area as a reserve in 1965 and in recent years the organisation has done a great deal to create new paths through the woods and along the harbour edge. You don't really need a guidebook here at all – simply follow the waymarked trails at will (not forgetting the recently opened route south across Coombe Heath to the edge of Middlebere Lake). For the record, however, this walk takes you along the longest of the RSPB's waymarked trails, marked at the time of writing with red squirrel waymarks.

THE WALK

Leave the car park, turning right just past the information centre to take a woodland path. This is a pleasant stroll which takes you directly to the heart of the reserve. After a while, the path bends to the left and then meets up with another path; turn right here, and carry on down towards the salt-flats at the edge of Poole Harbour These salt-marshes are a familiar sight at the outer reaches of the Harbour, and are dominated by spartina grass, which spreads over nearly 2,000 acres of mud-flats.

Ahead are two of Poole Harbour's islands, Round Island and Long Island, which spartina grass is busy trying to join into one. The Purbeck side of Poole Harbour is remote, and gives the appearance of being completely undeveloped, though underneath the heathland and harbour waters is the largest on-shore oil field in Europe.

Across the harbour lies Poole: the contrast between the two sides of the harbour could not be greater.

Follow the path which runs alongside the foreshore and then makes its way to the top of little Shipstal Hill. Here a plaque points out various landmarks. Turn away from the harbour and drop down the other side of the hill. At a meeting of paths, keep straight ahead following the sign to the hide.

The path enters woodland, skirting some stagnant pools where dragonflies can sometimes be seen. At a junction of paths, keep right until you reach the RSPB hide.

The bird hide looks out over the marshes of Arne Bay and the waters of Wareham channel. As the RSPB make clear, mud matters: this area of the harbour is a wonderful habitat for the waders and wildfowl. The redshank is the only breeding species of the saltmarshes, but shelducks nest nearby and their ducklings are a familiar sight on the mudflats in the breeding season. Depending on the time of year visitors to Shipstal may see, for example, avocets, red-breasted mergansers, goldeneyes, pintails, teal, black-tailed godwits and great crested grebes. Spoonbills have also been seen in the Arne area of the harbour in recent years.

It's also worth bird-watching in the woodland areas, where green and great spotted woodpeckers can be seen. Roe deer are frequent visitors, and there is no shortage of Sika, an Asian deer which originally escaped from a herd on Brownsea Island.

Arne Nature Trail

After leaving the hide continue briefly straight ahead, then turn right and shortly right again. This path leads you round the northern end of the reserve, into Big Wood, before bending back to reach the fields of Arne Farm. You emerge by the farm buildings in the centre of the village.

Arne is really nothing more than the church, a farm and a handful of cottages. The church, like those at Studland, Worth and Kimmeridge, is dedicated to St Nicholas, and dates from the late twelfth or early thirteenth century. It is a simple building and the main part of the church is still candle-lit.

Turn left by the church, and return along the road to the RSPB car park.

THE DOVECOTE PRESS

*publishes a wide range of illustrated books about Dorset,
of which the following may be of interest to anyone
wishing to know more about the Isle of Purbeck.*

Purbeck, The Ingrained Island
Paul Hyland   £4.95

Purbeck, A Portrait in Colour
David Burnett & David Bailey   £2.99

Tyneham, A Lost Heritage
Lilian Bond   £5.95

Dorset, The Complete Guide
Jo Draper   £12.95

and in the Discover Dorset series

Isle of Purbeck
Paul Hyland   £4.95

Coast & Sea
Sarah Welton   £5.95

Heathlands
Lesley Haskins   £5.95

Shipwrecks
Maureen Attwooll   £4.95

Geology
Paul Ensom   £4.95

Fossils
Richard Edmonds   £4.95

Stone Quarrying
Jo Thomas   £4.95